INTERACTIVE WHITEBOARD ACTIVITIES

Grades 4–6

P9-DEE-343

Math
LESSONS FOR THE SMART BOARD™

Motivating, Interactive Lessons That Teach Key Math Skills

■SCHOLASTIC

New York ○ Toronto ○ London ○ Auckland ○ Sydney
New Delhi ○ Mexico City ○ Hong Kong ○ Buenos Aires

Teaching *Resources*

Scholastic Inc. grants teachers permission to photocopy the reproducible pages from this book for classroom use. Purchase of this book entitles use of reproducibles by one teacher for one classroom only. No other part of this publication may be reproduced in whole or in part, or stored in a retrieval system, or transmitted in any form or by any means, electronic, mechanical, photocopying, recording, or otherwise, without written permission of the publisher. For information regarding permission, write to Scholastic Inc., 557 Broadway, New York, NY 10012.

Authors: Ann Montague-Smith, Anthony David, Linda Best
Illustrators: Jim Peacock, William Gray, Theresa Tibbetts, Andy Keylock, Garry Davies
Editor: Maria L. Chang
Cover design: Brian LaRossa
Interior design: Grafica Inc.

CD-ROM developed in association with Q & D Multimedia

Special thanks to Robin Hunt and Melissa Rugless of Scholastic Ltd.

SMART Board™ and Notebook™ are registered trademarks of SMART Technologies Inc.
Microsoft Office, Word, and Excel are either registered trademarks or trademarks of Microsoft Corporation in the United States and/or other countries.

All Flash activities designed and developed by Q & D Multimedia.

Interactive Teaching Programs (developed by the Primary National Strategy) © Crown copyright.

ISBN: 978-0-545-29045-6
Copyright © 2011 by Scholastic Inc.
All rights reserved.
Printed in the U.S.A.

2 3 4 5 6 7 8 9 10   40   18 17 16 15 14 13 12 11

Contents

Introduction

Interactive whiteboards are fast becoming the must-have resource in today's classroom as they allow teachers to facilitate children's learning in ways that were inconceivable a few years ago. The appropriate use of interactive whiteboards, whether used daily in the classroom or once a week in a computer lab, encourages active participation in lessons and increases students' determination to succeed. Interactive whiteboards make it easier for teachers to bring subjects across the curriculum to life in new and exciting ways.

What can an interactive whiteboard offer?

For teachers, an interactive whiteboard allows them to do the same things they can on an ordinary whiteboard, such as drawing, writing, and erasing. However, the interactive whiteboard also offers many other possibilities, such as:

- saving any work created during a lesson;
- preparing as many pages as necessary;
- displaying any page within the Notebook™ file to review teaching and learning;
- adding scanned examples of children's work to a Notebook file;
- changing colors of shapes and backgrounds instantly;
- using simple templates and grids;
- linking Notebook files to spreadsheets, Web sites, and presentations.

Using an interactive whiteboard in the simple ways outlined above can enrich teaching and learning in a classroom, but that is only the beginning of the whiteboard's potential to educate and inspire.

For students, the interactive whiteboard provides the opportunity to share learning experiences, as lessons can be delivered with sound, still and moving images, and Web sites. Interactive whiteboards can be used to cater to the needs of all learning styles:

- Kinesthetic learners benefit from being able to physically manipulate images.
- Visual learners benefit from being able to watch videos, look at photographs, and see images being manipulated.
- Auditory learners benefit from being able to access audio resources, such as voice recordings and sound effects.

With a little preparation, all of these resource types could be integrated into one lesson—a feat that would have been almost impossible before the advent of the interactive whiteboard!

Access to an interactive whiteboard

In schools where students have limited access to an interactive whiteboard, carefully planned lessons will help students get the most benefit from it during the times they can use it. As teachers become familiar with the interactive whiteboard, they will learn when to use it and, equally important, when not to use it!

Where permanent access to an interactive whiteboard is available, it is important to plan the use of the board effectively. It should be used only in ways that will enhance or extend teaching and learning. Children still need to gain practical, firsthand experience of many things. Some experiences cannot be recreated on an interactive whiteboard, but others cannot be had without it. *Math Lessons for the SMART Board*™ offers both teachers and learners the most accessible and creative uses of this most valuable resource.

About the book

Adapted from Scholastic UK's best-selling 100 SMART Board™ Lessons series, *Math Lessons for the SMART Board*™ is designed to reflect best practice in using interactive whiteboards. It is also designed to support all teachers in using this valuable tool by providing lessons and other resources that can be used on the SMART Board with little or no preparation. These inspirational lessons meet the Common Core State Standards for Mathematics and the National Council of Teachers of Math (NCTM) standards and are perfect for all levels of experience.

This book is divided into five chapters. Each chapter contains lessons covering:

- Number & Operations
- Algebra Readiness
- Measurement
- Geometry
- Data Analysis

Mini-Lessons

The mini-lessons have a consistent structure that includes:

- a **Getting Started** activity;
- a step-by-step **Mini-Lesson** plan;
- an **Independent Work** activity; and
- a **Wrap-Up** activity to round up the teaching and learning and identify any assessment opportunities.

Each mini-lesson identifies any resources required (including Notebook files that are provided on the CD-ROM, as well as reproducible activity pages) and lists the whiteboard tools that could be used in the mini-lesson.

The reproducible activity sheets toward the back of the book support the mini-lessons. These sheets provide opportunities for group or individual work to be completed away from the board, while linking to the context of the whiteboard lesson. They also provide opportunities for whole-class discussions in which children present their work.

What's on the CD-ROM?

The accompanying CD-ROM provides an extensive bank of Notebook files designed for use with the SMART Board. These support, and are supported by, the mini-lessons in this book. They can be annotated and saved for reference or for use with subsequent lessons; they can also be printed out. In addition to texts and images, a selection of Notebook files include the following types of files:

- **Embedded Microsoft PowerPoint and Excel files:** The embedded files are launched from the Notebook file and will open in their native Microsoft application.
- **Embedded interactive files:** These include specially commissioned interactive files that will open in a new browser window within the Notebook environment.
- **Embedded audio files:** Some Notebook files contain buttons that play sounds.
- **"Build Your Own" file:** This contains a blank Notebook page with a bank of selected images and interactive tools from the Gallery, as well as specially commissioned images. You can use this to help build your own Notebook files.

The Notebook files

All of the Notebook files have a consistent structure as follows:

- **Title and objectives page**—Use this page to highlight the focus of the mini-lesson. You might also wish to refer to this page at certain times throughout the lesson or at the end of the lesson to assess whether the learning objective was achieved.
- **Getting Started activity**—This sets the context of the lesson and usually provides some key questions or learning points that will be addressed through the main activities.
- **Main activities**—These activities offer independent, collaborative group, or whole-class work. The activities draw on the full scope of Notebook software and the associated tools, as well as on the SMART Board tools. "What to Do" boxes are also included in many of the prepared Notebook files. These appear as tabs in the top right-hand corner of the screen. To access these notes, simply pull out the tabs to reveal planning information, additional support, and key learning points.
- **Wrap-Up**—A whole-class activity or summary page is designed to review work done both at the board and away from the board. In many lessons, children are encouraged to present their work.

How to Use the CD-ROM

Setting up your screen for optimal use

It is best to view the Notebook pages at a screen display setting of 1280 x 1024 pixels. To alter the screen display, select Settings, then Control Panel from the Start menu. Next, double-click on the Display icon, then click on the Settings tab. Finally, adjust the Screen Area scroll bar to 1280 x 1024 pixels. Click on OK. (On the Mac, click on the apple icon and select System Preferences. Then click on Displays and select 1280 x 1024.)

If you prefer to use a screen display setting of 800 x 600 pixels, ensure that your Notebook view is set to "Page Width." To alter the view, launch Notebook and click on View. Go to Zoom and select the "Page Width" setting. If you use a screen display setting of 800 x 600 pixels, text in the prepared Notebook files may appear larger when you edit it on screen.

Getting started

The program should run automatically when you insert the CD-ROM into your CD drive. If it does not, use My Computer to browse to the contents of the CD-ROM and click on the Scholastic icon. (On the Mac, click on the Scholastic icon to start the program.)

Main menu

The Main menu divides the Notebook files by topic: Number & Operations; Algebra Readiness; Measurement; Geometry; and Data Analysis. Clicking on the appropriate button for any of these options will take you to a separate Lessons menu. (See below for further information.) The "Build Your Own" file is also accessed through the Main menu.

Individual Notebook files or pages can be located using the search facility by keying in words (or part of words) from the resource titles in the Search box. Press Go to begin the search. This will bring up a list of the titles that match your search.

Lessons menu

Each Lessons menu provides all of the prepared Notebook files for each chapter of the book. Click on the buttons to open the Notebook files. Click on Main menu button to return to the Main menu screen. (To alternate between the menus on the CD-ROM and other open applications, hold down the Alt key and press the Tab key to switch to the desired application.)

"Build Your Own" file

Click on this button to open a blank Notebook page and a collection of Gallery objects, which will be saved automatically into the My Content folder in the Gallery. (Under My Content, open the Year 3 Folder, then the Math folder to access the Gallery objects.) You only need to click on this button the first time you wish to access the "Build Your Own" file, as the Gallery objects will remain in the My Content folder on the computer on which the file was opened. To use the facility again, simply open a blank Notebook page and access the images and interactive resources from the same folder under My Content. If you are using the CD-ROM on a different computer, you will need to click on the "Build Your Own" button again.

Safety note: Avoid looking directly at the projector beam as it is potentially damaging to the eyes, and never leave children unsupervised when using the interactive whiteboard.

Connections to the Math Standards

The mini-lessons and activities in this book meet the following Common Core State Standards for Mathematics and the National Council of Teachers of Mathematics (NCTM) Standards:

	COMMON CORE STATE STANDARDS	NCTM STANDARDS
NUMBER & OPERATIONS		
Place Value	**4.NBT.2:** Read and write multi-digit whole numbers using base-ten numerals, number names, and expanded form.	• Understand the place-value structure of the base-ten number system and be able to represent and compare whole numbers and decimals. • Recognize equivalent representations for the same number and generate them by decomposing and composing numbers.
Estimating and Approximating	**4.NBT.3:** Use place value understanding to round multi-digit whole numbers to any place.	• Recognize equivalent representations for the same number and generate them by decomposing and composing numbers.
Make 100	**4.NBT.4:** Fluently add and subtract multi-digit whole numbers using the standard algorithm.	• Develop fluency in adding, subtracting, multiplying, and dividing whole numbers.
Positive and Negative Numbers	**6.NS.5:** Understand that positive and negative numbers are used together to describe quantities having opposite directions or values; use positive and negative numbers to represent quantities in real-world contexts, explaining the meaning of 0 in each situation. **6.NS.6a:** Recognize opposite signs of numbers as indicating locations on opposite sides of 0 on the number line.	• Explore numbers less than 0 by extending the number line and through familiar applications. • Develop fluency in adding, subtracting, multiplying, and dividing whole numbers.
Common Multiples	**4.OA.4:** Find all factor pairs for a whole number in the range of 1–100. Recognize that a whole number is a multiple of each of its factors. Determine whether a given whole number in the range of 1–100 is a multiple of a given one-digit number. Determine whether a given whole number in the range of 1–100 is prime or composite. **6.NS.4:** Find the greatest common factor of two whole numbers less than or equal to 100 and the least common multiple of two whole numbers less than or equal to 12.	• Understand various meanings of multiplication and division. • Develop fluency with basic number combinations for multiplication and division and use these combinations to mentally compute related problems, such as 30 x 50. • Develop fluency in adding, subtracting, multiplying, and dividing whole numbers. • Use factors, multiples, prime factorization, and relatively prime number numbers to solve problems.
Fraction Machines	n/a	• Develop understanding of fractions as parts of unit wholes, such as parts of a collection, as locations on number lines, and as divisions of whole numbers. • Use models, benchmarks, and equivalent forms to judge the size of fractions.
Fraction Pizzas	**4.NF.1:** Explain why a fraction a/b is equivalent to a fraction $(n \times a) / (n \times b)$ by using visual fraction models, with attention to how the number and size of the parts differ even though the two fractions themselves are the same size. Use this principle to recognize and generate equivalent fractions. **4.NF.3d:** Solve word problems involving addition and subtraction of fractions referring to the same whole and having like denominators, e.g., by using visual fraction models and equations to represent the problem. **4.NF.4a:** Understand a fraction a/b as a multiple of $1/b$. **5.NF.3:** Interpret a fraction as division of the numerator by the denominator ($a/b = a \div b$). Solve word problems involving division of whole numbers leading to answers in the form of fractions or mixed numbers, e.g., by using visual fraction models or equations to represent the problem.	• Develop understanding of fractions as parts of unit wholes, such as parts of a collection, as locations on number lines, and as divisions of whole numbers. • Use models, benchmarks, and equivalent forms to judge the size of fractions.
Simplify Fractions	**4.NF.1:** Explain why a fraction a/b is equivalent to a fraction $(n \times a) / (n \times b)$ by using visual fraction models, with attention to how the number and size of the parts differ even though the two fractions themselves are the same size. Use this principle to recognize and generate equivalent fractions. **4.NF.4a:** Understand a fraction a/b as a multiple of $1/b$. **6.NS.4:** Find the greatest common factor of two whole numbers less than or equal to 100 and the least common multiple of two whole numbers less than or equal to 12.	• Develop understanding of fractions as parts of unit wholes, such as parts of a collection, as locations on number lines, and as divisions of whole numbers. • Recognize and generate equivalent forms of commonly used fractions, decimals, and percents.
Equivalent Fractions and Decimals	**4.NF.6:** Use a decimal notation for fractions with denominators 10 or 100.	• Develop understanding of fractions as parts of unit wholes, such as parts of a collection, as locations on number lines, and as divisions of whole numbers. • Use models, benchmarks, and equivalent forms to judge the size of fractions. • Recognize and generate equivalent forms of commonly used fractions, decimals, and percents.
Place Value of Decimal Numbers	**5.NBT.3:** Read, write, and compare decimals to thousandths.	• Understand the place-value structure of the base-ten number system and be able to represent and compare whole numbers and decimals.
Multiplying Decimals by 10, 100, and 1,000	**5.NBT.2:** Explain patterns in the number of zeros of the product when multiplying a number by powers of 10, and explain patterns in the placement of the decimal point when a decimal is multiplied or divided by a power of 10.	• Understand various meanings of multiplication and division. • Develop and use strategies to estimate computations involving fractions and decimals in situations relevant to students' experience. • Understand the meaning and effects of arithmetic operations with fractions, decimals, and integers.

Lying Between Decimals	**4.NF.7:** Compare two decimals to hundredths by reasoning about their size.	• Compare and order fractions, decimals, and percents efficiently and find their approximate locations on a number line.
Ordering and Rounding Decimals	**4.NF.7:** Compare two decimals to hundredths by reasoning about their size. **5.NBT.4:** Use place value understanding to round decimals to any place.	• Compare and order fractions, decimals, and percents efficiently and find their approximate locations on a number line.
Percentages, Parts 1 and 2	**6.RP.3c:** Find a percent of a quantity as a rate per 100 (e.g., 30% of a quantity means 30/100 times the quantity); solve problems involving finding the whole, given a part and the percent.	• Work flexibly with fractions, decimals, and percents to solve problems.

ALGEBRA READINESS

Solving Word Problems; Superheroes; More Superheroes	**4.OA.3:** Solve multistep word problems posed with whole numbers and having whole-number answers using the four operations, including problems in which remainders must be interpreted. Represent these problems using equations with a letter standing for the unknown quantity. Assess the reasonableness of answers using mental computation and estimation strategies including rounding.	• Represent the idea of a variable as an unknown quantity using a letter or a symbol. • Express mathematical relationships using equations. • Identify and use relationships between operations, such as division as the inverse of multiplication, to solve problems. • Understand and use properties of operations, such as the distributivity of multiplication over addition. • Develop fluency in adding, subtracting, multiplying, and dividing whole numbers.
Numbers and Shapes; Number Patterns	**4.OA.5:** Generate a number or shape pattern that follows a given rule. **5.OA.3:** Generate two numerical patterns using two given rules. Identify apparent relationships between corresponding terms.	• Describe, extend, and make generalizations about geometric and numeric patterns. • Represent, analyze, and generalize a variety of patterns with tables, graphs, words, and when possible, symbolic rules.

MEASUREMENT

Telling Time; Movie Times	**4.MD.1:** Know relative sizes of measurement units within one system of units including hr, min, sec. Within a single system of measurement, express measurements in a larger unit in terms of a smaller unit. Record measurement equivalents in a two-column table. **4.MD.2:** Use the four operations to solve word problems involving intervals of time including problems that require expressing measurements given in a larger unit in terms of a smaller unit.	• Select and apply appropriate standard units and tools to measure length, area, volume, weight, time, temperature, and the size of angles.
Ratio Problems	**6.RP.1:** Understand the concept of a ratio and use ratio language to describe a ratio relationship between two quantities. **6.RP.3:** Use ratio and rate reasoning to solve real-world and mathematical problems. **6.RP.3d:** Use ratio reasoning to convert measurement units; manipulate and transform units appropriately when multiplying or dividing quantities.	• Understand and use ratios and proportions to represent quantitative relationships. • Solve problems involving scale factors, using ratio and proportion. • Develop, analyze, and explain methods for solving problems involving proportions, such as scaling and finding equivalent ratios.
Measuring; Metric Units of Measurement; Suitable Units of Measurement; Customary Units of Measurement	**4.MD.1:** Know relative sizes of measurement units within one system of units including km, m, cm; kg, g; lb, oz.; l, ml. Within a single system of measurement, express measurements in a larger unit in terms of a smaller unit. **5.MD.1:** Convert among different-sized standard measurement units within a given measurement system, and use these conversions in solving multi-step, real world problems.	• Understand such attributes as length, area, weight, volume, and size of angle and select the appropriate type of unit for measuring each attribute. • Understand the need for measuring with standard units and become familiar with standard units in the customary and metric systems. • Carry out simple unit conversions, such as from centimeters to meters, within a system of measurement. • Understand that measurements are approximations and understand how differences in units affect precision. • Select and apply appropriate standard units and tools to measure length, area, volume, weight, time, temperature, and the size of angles. • Understand both metric and customary systems of measurement. • Understand relationships among units and convert from one unit to another within the same system.
Crazy Quads; Polygon Puzzles; Perimeter Challenge	**4.MD.3:** Apply the area and perimeter formulas for rectangles in real world and mathematical problems. **6.G.1:** Find the area of right triangles, other triangles, special quadrilaterals, and polygons by composing into rectangles or decomposing into triangles and other shapes; apply these techniques in the context of solving real-world and mathematical problems.	• Explore what happens to measurements of a two-dimensional shape such as its perimeter and area when the shape is changed in some way. • Develop strategies for estimating the perimeters, areas, and volumes of irregular shapes. • Develop, understand, and use formulas to find the area of rectangles and related triangles and parallelograms.

GEOMETRY

Polygons	**4.G.2:** Classify two-dimensional figures based on the presence or absence of parallel or perpendicular lines, or the presence or absence of angles of a specified size. Recognize right triangles as a category, and identify right triangles. **5.G.3:** Understand that attributes belonging to a category of two-dimensional figures also belong to all subcategories of that category. **5.G.4:** Classify two-dimensional figures in a hierarchy based on properties.	• Identify, compare, and analyze attributes of two- and three-dimensional shapes and develop vocabulary to describe the attributes. • Classify two- and three-dimensional shapes according to their properties and develop definitions of classes of shapes such as triangles and pyramids.
Reflections; Mirror Shapes	**4.G.3:** Recognize a line of symmetry for a two-dimensional figure as a line across the figure such that the figure can be folded along the line into matching parts. Identify line-symmetric figures and draw lines of symmetry.	• Predict and describe the results of sliding, flipping, and turning two-dimensional shapes. • Describe a motion or a series of motions that will show that two shapes are congruent. • Identify and describe line and rotational symmetry in two- and three-dimensional shapes and designs. • Describe sizes, positions, and orientations of shapes under informal transformations such as flips, turns, slides, and scaling. • Examine the congruence, similarity, and line or rotational symmetry of objects using transformations.

Rotation	n/a	• Predict and describe the results of sliding, flipping, and turning two-dimensional shapes. • Describe a motion or a series of motions that will show that two shapes are congruent. • Identify and describe line and rotational symmetry in two- and three-dimensional shapes and designs. • Describe sizes, positions, and orientations of shapes under informal transformations such as flips, turns, slides, and scaling. • Examine the congruence, similarity, and line or rotational symmetry of objects using transformations.
Identifying Angles; Acute and Obtuse Angles	**4.MD.5:** Recognize angles as geometric shapes that are formed wherever two rays share a common endpoint, and understand concepts of angle measurement. **4.MD.6:** Measure angles in whole-number degrees using a protractor. **4.G.1:** Draw points, lines, line segments, rays, angles (right, acute, obtuse), and perpendicular and parallel lines. Identify these in two-dimensional figures.	• Understand such attributes as length, area, weight, volume, and size of angle and select the appropriate type of unit for measuring each attribute. • Select and apply appropriate standard units and tools to measure length, area, volume, weight, time, temperature, and the size of angles.
The Sum of Angles	**4.MD.7:** Recognize angle measure as additive. When an angle is decomposed into non-overlapping parts, the angle measure of the whole is the sum of the angle measures of the parts. Solve addition and subtraction problems to find unknown angles on a diagram in real world and mathematical problems.	• Identify, compare, and analyze attributes of two- and three-dimensional shapes and develop vocabulary to describe the attributes. • Classify two- and three-dimensional shapes according to their properties and develop definitions of classes of shapes such as triangles and pyramids. • Select and apply appropriate standard units and tools to measure length, area, volume, weight, time, temperature, and the size of angles.
The Truth About Triangles	**4.G.2:** Classify two-dimensional figures based on the presence or absence of parallel or perpendicular lines, or the presence or absence of angles of a specified size. Recognize right triangles as a category, and identify right triangles. **5.G.3:** Understand that attributes belonging to a category of two-dimensional figures also belong to all subcategories of that category. **5.G.4:** Classify two-dimensional figures in a hierarchy based on properties.	• Identify, compare, and analyze attributes of two- and three-dimensional shapes and develop vocabulary to describe the attributes. • Classify two- and three-dimensional shapes according to their properties and develop definitions of classes of shapes such as triangles and pyramids. • Understand relationships among the angles, side lengths, perimeters, areas, and volumes of similar objects.
Nets	**6.G.4:** Represent three-dimensional figures using nets made up of rectangles. Apply these techniques in the context of solving real-world and mathematical problems.	• Identify and build a three-dimensional object from two-dimensional representations of that object. • Identify and draw a two-dimensional representation of a three-dimensional object.
3D Shapes	**6.G.4:** Represent three-dimensional figures using nets made up of rectangles. Apply these techniques in the context of solving real-world and mathematical problems.	• Classify two- and three-dimensional shapes according to their properties and develop definitions of classes of shapes such as triangles and pyramids. • Investigate, describe, and reason about the results of subdividing, combining, and transforming shapes. • Identify and build a three-dimensional object from two-dimensional representations of that object. • Identify and draw a two-dimensional representation of a three-dimensional object.
Finding Positions; Coordinates	**5.G.1:** Use a pair of perpendicular number lines, called axes, to define a coordinate system, with the intersection of the lines (the origin) arranged to coincide with the 0 on each line and a given point in the plane located by using an ordered pair of numbers, called its coordinates. Understand that the first number indicates how far to travel from the origin in the direction of one axis, and the second number indicates how far to travel in the direction of the second axis, with the convention that the names of the two axes and the coordinate correspond (e.g., x-axis and x-coordinate, y-axis and y-coordinate). **5.G.2:** Represent real world and mathematical problems by graphing points in the first quadrant of the coordinate plane, and interpret coordinate values of points in the context of the situation. **6.G.3:** Draw polygons in the coordinate plane given coordinates for the vertices; use coordinates to find the length of a side joining points with the same first coordinate or the same second coordinate. Apply these techniques in the context of solving real-world and mathematical problems.	• Describe location and movement using common language and geometric vocabulary. • Make and use coordinate systems to specify locations and to describe paths. • Find the distance between points along horizontal and vertical lines of a coordinate system. • Use coordinate geometry to represent and examine the properties of geometric shapes.

DATA ANALYSIS

Pictograms; Bar Charts	**6.SP.1:** Recognize a statistical question as one that anticipates variability in the data related to the question and accounts for it in the answers. **6.SP.2:** Understand that a set of data collected to answer a statistical question has a distribution, which can be described by its center, spread, and overall shape. **6.SP.4:** Display numerical data in plots on a number line, including dot plots, histograms, and box plots. **6.SP.5a:** Summarize numerical data sets in relation to their context, such as by reporting the number of observations. **6.SP.5b:** Summarize numerical data sets in relation to their context, such as by describing the nature of the attribute under investigation, including how it was measured and its units of measurement.	• Design investigations to address a question and consider how data-collection methods affect the nature of the data set. • Collect data using observations, surveys, and experiments. • Represent data using tables and graphs such as line plots, bar graphs, and line graphs.
Analyzing Data	**6.SP.5c:** Summarize numerical data sets in relation to their context, such as by describing the nature of the attribute under investigation, including how it was measured and its units of measurement. **6.SP.5c:** Summarize numerical data sets in relation to their context, such as by giving quantitative measures of center (median and/or mean) and variability (interquartile range and/or mean absolute deviation), as well as describing any overall pattern and any striking deviations from the overall pattern with reference to the context in which the data were gathered.	• Use measures of center, focusing on the median, and understand what each does and does not indicate about the data set • Find, use, and interpret measures of center and spread, including mean and interquartile range.

Place Value

Learning objective
- Expand and order four-digit whole numbers.

Resources
- "Place Value" Notebook file
- "A Place for Each Digit" (p. 56)
- individual whiteboards and pens
- a set of 0–9 number cards for each pair

Whiteboard tools
- Pen tray
- Select tool

Getting Started

Explain that you will say a whole number up to 1,000. Ask students to write it using numerals on their individual whiteboards and then show you. Write the whole number on page 2 of the "Place Value" Notebook file to confirm how it should be written. Invite a volunteer to write the same whole number in words on the Notebook page.

Repeat this process and include examples where zero is a placeholder for tens and/or ones, such as 650 or 605. Ask students questions such as: *What does the zero stand for? What digit is in the hundreds/tens/ones place?*

Mini-Lesson

1. Extend the number range from the Getting Started activity to include thousands. Write an example on page 3 of the Notebook file using figures and words, such as 4,256 and *four thousand two hundred and fifty-six.*

2. Provide further examples for students to try for themselves, such as 9,043 and 7,360. Extend to whole numbers greater than 10,000, writing an example on page 3. For each example, ask: *What does ___ stand for? Which place does the digit ___ hold?*

3. Display page 4 of the Notebook file. Ask a student to drag a number from the box at the bottom of the screen into the "Whole number" column in the table.

4. Invite students to suggest how to fill in each of the columns. Ask a volunteer to drag and drop each digit into place using the numbers at the bottom of the table. Repeat for seven more four-digit numbers dragged from the number box.

5. Use page 5 to investigate whole numbers greater than 10,000. This can be done as part of this lesson or in a later lesson.

Independent Work

Ask students to work in pairs. Provide each pair with a set of 0–9 numeral cards and a copy of "A Place for Each Digit" (p. 56). Have partners take turns picking four numeral cards so that both students make a four-digit whole number using the cards. They should try to make their integers different. Then have them record their whole number and each digit's place value on the reproducible sheet.

Decide whether or not to limit the range to three-digit integers for less-confident learners by blanking out the thousands column on the sheet. Challenge more-confident learners to extend the range to five-digit integers. They can draw their own table to complete the work.

Wrap-Up

Use page 6 of the Notebook file to invite students to take turns saying one of their whole numbers. Write their whole number in the "Whole number" column of the table. Invite other students to drag and drop, or write, the appropriate digits in the other place-value columns. Ask questions such as: *Which digit represents thousands/hundreds/tens/ones? What would the whole number be if you switched the tens and hundreds digits?*

Estimating and Approximating

Learning objective
- Use knowledge of rounding, number operations, and inverse operations to estimate and check calculations.

Resources
- "Estimating and Approximating" Notebook file
- transparent containers filled with between 100 and 250 counters
- paper plates
- paper and pencils

Whiteboard tools
- Pen tray
- Select tool
- Screen Shade
- Undo button

Getting Started

Display page 2 of the "Estimating and Approximating" Notebook file. Show the image for about five seconds and invite students to estimate how many counters there are. Hide the screen with the Screen Shade. Ask students to record their estimates on their individual whiteboards and invite them to share their estimates.

Reveal the screen again and ask: *How shall we count these to check?* Invite a student to demonstrate by counting in fives or tens. The counters can be dragged and grouped into sets. Reveal the answer at the top of the page. Use the Undo button until the page is reset and delete some of the counters. Repeat the estimating activity.

Mini-Lesson

1. Display page 3 of the Notebook file. Ask: *How many stars do you estimate are there? How did you make your estimate?* Ask students to write their prediction of the number of objects on their individual whiteboards.

2. Invite a student to demonstrate how they made their estimate, such as counting a small number of stars and multiplying.

3. Repeat this for pages 4 and 5.

4. Now show students the prepared containers with counters (see Resources). Tell them to work in small groups to estimate how many counters there are. Allow about five minutes for this.

5. Bring the class back together. Compare and discuss estimates and how these were made. Invite students to check their estimates by counting the counters in their container.

6. Hide the containers and remove half (or a quarter) of the counters from each. Show each container in turn and ask students to estimate about how many counters have been removed and to express this as a fraction.

Independent Work

Have students work in pairs and give each pair about 250 counters in a container, a large paper plate, and paper and pencils. Have partners take turns spreading out some of the counters on the plate. Partners should both estimate how many counters there are and record their estimate. Challenge students to think of a quick way to count the counters. Then have them record the actual number. Ask students to repeat the activity ten times.

Limit the maximum number of counters to 100 for less-confident learners. Challenge more-confident learners by increasing the number to 300.

Wrap-Up

Display page 6 of the Notebook file and ask students to estimate how many triangles are on the page. Invite them to explain how they figured this out. Repeat for page 7. Invite a student to estimate half of the circles on page 7 by selecting approximately half of the circles and deleting them. Then ask another student to estimate half of what is left in the same way. Ask: *What portion is left?* (A quarter) *Do you agree? Why do you think that?* Repeat for other quantities, asking students to remove estimates of quarters and halves.

Make 100

Learning objective

- Use knowledge of addition and subtraction facts and place value to derive sums and differences of pairs of multiples of 10, 100, or 1,000.

Resources

- "Make 100" Notebook file
- "Add Up to 100" (p. 57)
- two different-colored pencils for each pair of students

Whiteboard tools

- Pen tray
- Pen tool
- Select tool

Getting Started

Explain that you will say a small number. Ask students to call out together the number that adds to your number to make a total of 20. So, for example, if you say 13, students should call out 7. Keep a good pace to encourage rapid recall.

Alternatively, you can drag random numbers from the Numbers box on page 2 of the "Make 100" Notebook file if students find it easier to see the number. If students falter for any responses, reveal the hundred grid on the *Number Grid Interactive Teaching Program* and use this to demonstrate the answer by counting up to the target number.

Mini-Lesson

1. Go to page 3 of the Notebook file and explain to students that they will be finding pairs of numbers that add up to 100, quickly and easily.

2. Begin with the easier pairs, using what is already known: 9 + 1 = 10; 90 + 10 = 100, and so on. Press on the pairs in the hundred grid to highlight and mark these numbers so that students can see which pairs have been found. Use the Pen tool to change the colors of the paired numbers for easy identification.

3. Now move to other pairs, asking students: *How did you figure out the answer?* Praise those students who "knew" it. Spend about five minutes on finding other pairs.

Independent Work

Ask students to work in pairs on "Add Up to 100" (p. 57). Invite students to take turns choosing a start number for their partner. The partner finds the other number that adds up to 100. The first student can challenge if he or she thinks the partner is wrong, and must find a way to demonstrate that he or she is correct. Students score a point for a correct answer. Encourage them to color each pair of numbers, each student using a different color. They should continue until they have found all pairs.

Work with less-confident learners as a group. Invite them to take turns saying a pair of numbers they think totals 100. Discuss strategies for finding answers. When the more-confident learners have finished playing the game, ask them to write some strategies for finding solutions quickly.

Wrap-Up

Go to page 4 of the Notebook file and put the class into four teams. Appoint a captain for each team and play "Finding pairs to make 100" as a class game. Invite the more-confident learners to suggest strategies for finding solutions quickly. List these strategies on page 4, and invite all students to think of which pairs could be made using that strategy. Strategies could include: using decade numbers, using numbers that end in 5, and using addition facts to 10 to find the ones digit of the missing number.

Positive and Negative Numbers

Learning objective
- Find the difference between a positive and a negative integer, or two negative integers, in context.

Resources
- "Positive and Negative Numbers" Notebook file
- "Dice Template (p. 58)
- individual whiteboards and pens
- math notebooks

Whiteboard tools
- Pen tray
- Select tool

Getting Started
Show students the thermometer on page 2 of the "Positive and Negative Numbers" Notebook file. Invite individuals to come to the SMART Board to identify points on the thermometer, such as negative 20 degrees, by dragging the temperature gauge. Uncheck the "Hide temperature" box to see if they are right. Discuss the vocabulary used to identify differences in temperature and write the words around the thermometer (for example: *above zero, below zero, integer, positive, negative, minus*).

Focus on the order of the numbers on the thermometer and, if necessary, draw a separate number line underneath the thermometer to highlight the position of each integer.

Mini-Lesson
1. Work through pages 3 to 10 of the Notebook file with students. Invite individual students to come to the SMART Board to move the balloons on each page into the correct order. Alternatively, ask students to write the correct order on their individual whiteboards.

2. When they have done this, use the Eraser from the Pen tray to reveal the correct order on each page.

3. Remind students of the position of the numbers on the thermometer in the Getting Started activity. Show the thermometer on page 11 and point out the difference between two temperatures. Use the number line to work out the difference.

4. Work through pages 12 to 17 of the Notebook file. Ask students to look at the two numbers on each page and find the difference between each pair.

5. Invite individual students to use a Pen from the Pen tray to write their answers on the Notebook page, using the number line for assistance. After they have done this, ask them to use the Eraser to reveal the answers.

6. Encourage students to pay particular attention to whether the number is positive or negative.

Independent Work
Arrange students into small groups. Use the blank "Dice Template" (p. 58) to give each group a die with numbers between −25 and +25. Invite students to take turns rolling the die twice and writing the difference between the two numbers, using blank number lines in their math notebooks.

Provide less-confident learners with dice with numbers between −15 and +15. Provide more-confident learners with dice with numbers between −35 and +35.

Wrap-Up
Discuss the methods that students used, including any problems they might have experienced and what they found easy. Note these on page 18 of the Notebook file. Encourage students to think about how they can overcome their difficulties. Use pages 19 and 20 to reinforce ordering positive and negative numbers.

Common Multiples

* Use knowledge of multiplication facts to 10 x 10 to derive related multiplication facts.

Resources
* "Common Multiples" Notebook file
* individual whiteboards and pens
* five-sided spinners (with the digits 2, 3, 4, 5, and 10)
* eight-sided dice or spinners (with the digits 2, 3, 4, 5, 6, 7, 8, and 10)
* 11-sided dice or spinners (with the digits 2 to 12)
* writing materials

Whiteboard tools
* Pen tray
* Select tool

Getting Started

Ask students for the definition of a *multiple*. Write suggestions on the SMART Board (if necessary, reveal the prepared definition on page 2 of the "Common Multiples" Notebook file). Discuss any misconceptions at this stage.

Press the dice on the page to roll them. Ask students to put the numbers together in either order (for example, dice rolls 3 and 2 = 32 or 23). Have them write any multiples of the number on paper or on their individual whiteboards.

Review the multiples and then repeat up to three times. Ask: *Did we make any numbers that had no factors?* (For example, 11) *What are these numbers called?* (Prime numbers)

Mini-Lesson

1. Invite the class to identify multiples on pages 3 to 12 of the Notebook file by voting which of the four choices (*a*, *b*, *c*, or *d*) is the correct answer. For example, you might ask students to vote on each answer by putting up their hand or by writing on their individual whiteboards.

2. Ask volunteers to write the number that is a multiple of the given number at the top of the page.

3. Allow about 15 seconds for students to answer each question. Press on the answer to hear an audio indication of whether or not it is correct. You will hear a cheer for a correct answer or a groan for an incorrect one.

4. For each question, ask students to identify the other number that is required to make the multiple.

Independent Work

Divide the class into small groups. Show students page 13 of the Notebook file. Provide each group with a selection of dice or spinners (see Resources). In their groups, students use an eight-sided die or spinner with the digits 2, 3, 4, 5, 6, 7, 8, and 10. Ask them to write the first five multiples for the number they have landed on. As a variation, ask them to play as above but to roll the die/spinner a second time. For example, if a 5 is rolled, students must start from the fifth multiple of the first number rolled. Ask students to record the starting numbers and the five multiples on paper.

For less-confident learners, limit the activity to a five-sided spinner with the numbers 2, 3, 4, 5, and 10. Again, ask students to spin the spinner and write the first five multiples for the number they have spun. Provide more-confident learners with an 11-sided spinner with the same numbers as the eight-sided spinner, plus 9, 11, and 12.

Wrap-Up

Review the Independent Work, focusing on any particular areas of difficulty. Notes can be made on page 14 of the Notebook file. If time is available, roll two or four dice. Invite students to put two or more numbers together and write any multiples of that number on whiteboards. Alternatively, they could add or subtract numbers to make their starting numbers for this activity. You can find additional multiples questions for reinforcing this activity on pages 15 to 24 of the Notebook file.

Fraction Machines

Learning objective

- Express a smaller whole number as a fraction of a larger one (e.g., recognize that 5 out of 8 is $\frac{5}{8}$).

Resources

- "Fraction Machines" Notebook file
- individual whiteboards and pens

Whiteboard tools

- Pen tray
- Select tool
- Gallery

Getting Started

Display page 2 of the "Fraction Machines" Notebook file. Ask: *What pairs of factors make the number in the circle?* Use the Eraser from the Pen tray to reveal the factors in the smaller circles. Repeat for pages 3 and 4. There are only two factors for the final number because 51 is a prime number and can be divided only by 1 and itself.

Mini-Lesson

1. Go to page 5 of the Notebook file and ask a volunteer to say a fraction. Create it on the Notebook page using the Fraction Maker. (To use the Fraction Maker, use a Pen from the Pen tray to write the numerator and denominator and then press the arrow to create the fraction.) Repeat two or three times. Ask the class to think of as many different fractions as they can, writing them on their whiteboards. Warn them that they must be able to read the fraction correctly to their partner for the next part of the exercise.

2. Go to page 6. Can students remember the names of the two number parts of a fraction? Discuss before revealing the names and definitions by pressing the box at the top of the page.

3. Pair up students and ask one student in each pair to select a fraction from their partner's list. The other student has to name it. If the answerer can't name it, the questioner gets a point; if the answerer can name it, the answerer gets a point.

4. Move around the classroom as students play, spotting problems. Discuss any common disagreements and make general class rules. Ask volunteers to write a fraction on the board and challenge the whole class to say it.

5. Go to page 7. Explain to students that the Fraction Machine converts mixed numbers into *improper fractions* (fractions in which the numerator is larger than the denominator). Remind the class of the definition for a *denominator*. As an example, show students that $3\text{-}\frac{1}{3}$ is equal to the sum:

$$\left(3 \times \frac{3}{3}\right) + \frac{1}{3} \;=\; \frac{(3 \times 3) + 1}{3} \;=\; \frac{10}{3}$$

6. Ask students to figure out what the improper fraction is for the first example. Drag the fraction over to the other side of the machine to reveal the answer. Repeat for the other fractions.

Independent Work

Have students randomly pick a whole number and pair it with a common fraction, such as $\frac{1}{2}$ or $\frac{1}{4}$. They should then express this mixed number as an improper fraction. For example, $5\frac{1}{4} = \frac{21}{4}$.

Wrap-Up

Go to page 8 of the Notebook file and ask students to show how they created their fraction from the mixed number that they started with. Review the terms *denominator* and *numerator* and identify any misconceptions.

Fraction Pizzas

Learning objective
- Express a smaller whole number as a fraction of a larger one (e.g., recognize that 5 out of 8 is $5/8$).

Resources
- "Fraction Pizzas" Notebook file
- individual whiteboards and pens

Whiteboard tools
- Pen tray
- Select tool
- Calculator (from the SMART Board Tools menu)

Getting Started
Write six whole numbers on page 2 of the "Fraction Pizzas" Notebook file. Ask: *What products can you make by multiplying pairs of these numbers together?* Students should write calculations and answers on their individual whiteboards. Use the on-screen timer to impose a time limit.

Ask volunteers to write one multiplication fact and its answer on the board for the rest of the class to check. If the class is not sure, use the Calculator (from the SMART Board Tools menu) to confirm the answers.

Mini-Lesson
1. Remind students of their definitions for *numerator* and *denominator*.

2. Display page 3 of the Notebook file. Ask: *How many quarters of pizza are there?* (12 slices in three whole pizzas)

3. Explain that $12/4$ is an improper fraction (one in which the numerator is larger than the denominator). Copy and paste another pizza cut up into quarters. Ask: *How many quarters are there now?* ($16/4$) Repeat this with another pizza.

4. Go to page 4. Discuss methods to work out the pizza problems. (Suggestions may include adding four, counting on, or multiplying by four.)

5. Write up suggestions. Say that you want to test the multiplying rule.

6. Display page 5. The pizzas have now been cut into three equal pieces. Ask: *How many thirds will there be in all? How can you check this answer?* (There are 12 thirds because 4 x 3 = 12.)

7. Check the answer by doing the problem in reverse: Divide 12 by 3 to work out that there are 4 whole pizzas.

8. Display page 6 and ask students to work out the fraction number sentence for these pizzas. Repeat the activity for pages 7 and 8.

9. Go to page 9. Ask: *What happens if the answer is not a whole number? How could we find out how many whole pizzas there are in $11/5$ slices?* Compare answers and discuss. Extra copies of the pizza are available underneath the top image. The pizza can be divided into five equal slices by pressing on the image and dragging each slice away from the center.

Independent Work
Display page 10 of the Notebook file. Have students choose one number from each column to create an improper fraction ($12/5$ for example). Then have them put the class method to the test by using it to change the improper fraction back into a mixed number.

Wrap-Up
Ask students to use page 11 of the Notebook file to explain their work. Highlight good strategies. Explain that "chunking" can be used for large numbers, such as $523/5$. For example, there are 100 5s in 500, 4 in 20, which leaves $3/5$. The answer is therefore 104 $3/5$.

Simplify Fractions

Learning objective
- Simplify fractions by canceling common factors.

Resources
- "Simplify Fractions" Notebook file
- "Dice Template" (p. 58)
- individual whiteboards and pens, or math notebooks for recording

Whiteboard tools
- Pen tray
- Delete button
- Select tool
- Pen tool
- Gallery (Search for and use the Fraction Maker to generate fractions, if needed.)

Before You Start
Use the blank "Dice Template" (p. 58) to create three dice for each group of students. On each die, write fractions with the common factors of 2 or 5 (for less-confident learners); factors of 2, 5, 10, 3, and 4 (for middle-ability learners); and a variety of different factors (for more-confident learners).

Getting Started
Using pages 2 and 3 of the "Simplify Fractions" Notebook file, ask students to think about what a fraction is, what is meant by *simplest form*, and what they think a factor is. Encourage them to use vocabulary such as *numerator* and *denominator*. Record their responses on the Notebook pages and discuss any misconceptions.

Mini-Lesson
1. Go to page 4 of the Notebook file. Using this page, encourage students to explore what a factor is and how it can be used to cancel fractions down to their simplest form.

2. Ask students what number could be used to divide the numerator and the denominator. (2) Tell them that this is called a *common factor*. Delete the first panel to check the common factor for the example.

3. Now ask students to use this factor to find out how many times it goes into the numerator and denominator. Show students how to use the common factor to simplify the fraction $2/4$:

   2 divided by 2 is 1   4 divided by 2 is 2   so $1/2$ is a simplified form of $2/4$

   Delete the bottom panel to check the answer.

4. Page 5 can be used to reinforce the notion of equivalent fractions. Invite a student to use a Pen from the Pen tray to color in $2/4$ and $1/2$ of the shapes to demonstrate that the two fractions are the same, but that $1/2$ is the simplest form. (Select a fairly thick setting for the Pen via the Pen tool.)

5. Repeat the process for simplifying for the next four fractions on pages 6 to 9. Use the Eraser from the Pen tray to reveal the answers.

Independent Work
Give three fraction dice to each group, differentiated to suit students' abilities (see Before You Start). Ask students to roll the dice and record the fractions in their notebooks or on their individual whiteboards. Challenge them to reduce these fractions to their simplest forms.

Wrap-Up
Go to page 10 of the Notebook file. Discuss with students how they found the simplest form of a fraction. Use voting methods to take a tally of how easy or difficult they found the activity. For example, ask them to write a number from 1 to 6 on their whiteboards and then hold up their boards so that you can take a tally of the votes. Make a note of any difficulties on the Notebook page and work through the process of simplifying fractions as a whole class.

Equivalent Fractions and Decimals

Learning objective
- Find equivalent decimals and fractions.

Resources
- "Equivalent Fractions and Decimals" Notebook file
- "Matching Decimals and Fractions" (p. 59), copied onto cardstock
- individual whiteboards and pens

Whiteboard tools
- Pen tray
- Select tool
- Gallery (Search for and use the Fraction Maker to generate fractions, if needed.)

Getting Started

Establish the learning objective on page 1 of the "Equivalent Fractions and Decimals" Notebook file. Go to page 2. Working in ability groups, ask students to think about what the words *decimal* and *fraction* mean.

Invite the groups to share their ideas. Write their ideas on the Notebook page. Note that decimals and fractions are related because both are worked out from one whole.

Mini-Lesson

1. Work through the matching activities on pages 3 to 5 of the Notebook file. Discuss how students can figure out the equivalent fractions and decimals.

2. Provide students with individual whiteboards to figure out for themselves which fractions and decimals are equivalents.

3. Invite students to swap boards and to share their methods of figuring out with a partner.

4. Drag the equivalents next to each other on Notebook pages 3 to 5, discussing how students figured out each answer. Ask students to mark their partner's answers.

Independent Work

Keep students in their ability groups. Give each student a copy of "Matching Decimals and Fractions" (p. 59), printed on cardstock. (Alternatively, cut out and distribute the relevant sections to the different ability groups.)

Work with less-confident learners to complete the top section of the worksheet. Ask them to cut out the selection of fractions and decimals and match them to their equivalents. Help them figure out the solutions on the SMART Board, using page 6 of the Notebook file.

Have middle-ability groups complete the top and middle sections of the worksheet. They should cut out the selection of fractions and decimals and match them to their equivalents. Have students show their work on their own individual whiteboards.

Challenge more-confident learners to complete all three sections of the worksheet. Invite them to cut out the selection of fractions and decimals and match them to their equivalents. Ask them to show their work on their whiteboards.

Wrap-Up

Encourage students to discuss with their partners the method they used to check that the fractions and decimals were equivalent. Note students' ideas on page 7 of the Notebook file. Address any misconceptions. Use the *Fractions Interactive Teaching Program* to show fractions, decimals, percentages, and ratios alongside one another. Click on the arrows below the ÷ icon to set the number of parts the green bar should be divided. To set a fraction, click on each part to turn it yellow. Then click on the icon with the letters *f d p r* to show the fraction, decimal, percent, or ratio next to the bar.

Place Value of Decimal Numbers

Learning objective
- Use decimal notation for tenths, hundredths, and thousandths.

Resources
- "Place Value of Decimal Numbers" Notebook file
- "Dice Template" (p. 58)
- individual whiteboards and pens
- writing materials

Whiteboard tools
- Pen tray
- Select tool
- Highlighter pen

Before You Start

Use the blank "Dice Template" (p. 58) to create three dice for each group—one die with the digit positions 10ths, 100ths, and 1000ths (use 1s, 10s, 100s, 10ths, 100ths, and 1000ths for the higher-ability groups) and two dice with various numbers with up to three decimal places, differentiated to each group's ability. See page 5 of the "Place Value of Decimal Numbers" Notebook file for suggestions for the dice template.

Getting Started

Organize students into mixed-ability groups. Display page 2 of the "Place Value of Decimal Numbers" Notebook file. Ask students to think about decimal numbers and the different features of a decimal number. Using a Highlighter pen and Pen from the Pen tray, work with students to label the number's different parts—hundreds, tens, ones, decimal point, tenths, hundredths, and thousandths. Discuss any misunderstandings, then press the arrow at the bottom of the page to reveal the different parts of the decimal number.

Mini-Lesson

1. Go to page 3 of the Notebook file. Tell students that they will be asked a series of questions to identify the position of a digit in a number with up to three decimal places.

2. Press the thumbnail image to start the quiz. There are ten questions for students to answer. Read out each question and the possible answers. Count down from 15 to give students a time limit to answer each question. Encourage them to answer each question independently before deciding upon a class answer.

3. Provide less-confident learners with a word bank to help with their answers.

Independent Work

Give each group two number dice and one digit-position die (see Before You Start). Display page 4 of the Notebook file. Have students draw on paper a three-columned table with the headings "Number," "Digit Position," and "Digit." Invite students to do the following activity:

- Students roll one of the number dice to get a number with decimal places. They should record this number in the first column of the table.

- Next, they roll their digit-position die and record this position in the second column.

- Finally, students need to figure out which digit is in this position in the whole number. For example, if they roll 329.769 on the number die and 100th on their digit-position die, then they record 6 in the final column of the table.

  Provide a printout of the Notebook file's page 7 (the annotated decimal number) to ensure that they understand the different decimal positions.

Wrap-Up

Use the quiz on page 6 of the Notebook file to assess students' understanding of the place value of decimal numbers. Check any incorrect answers and discuss any misconceptions that may occur.

Multiplying Decimals by 10, 100, and 1,000

Learning objective
- Use knowledge of place value and multiplication facts to 10 x 10 to derive related multiplication facts involving decimals.

Resources
- "Multiplying Decimals by 10, 100, and 1000" Notebook file
- "Dice Template" (p. 58)
- individual whiteboards and pens

Whiteboard tools
- Pen tray
- Select tool

Before You Start
Use the blank "Dice Template" (p. 58) to create three dice for each student—one multiplier die with x10, x100, and x1,000 twice (replace one set of numbers with ÷10, ÷100, ÷1000 for more-confident learners) and two number dice with various numbers with up to three decimal places, differentiated to each group's ability.

Getting Started
Open page 2 of the "Multiplying Decimals by 10, 100, and 1,000" Notebook file. Press the image to the *Moving Digits Interactive Teaching Program* and use it to talk through the place value of each number in a decimal number. To create a decimal number, click on a number card at the top of the page, then drag that digit to the desired place value below. Repeat until you have the decimal number you want. Then click on the x10 or x100 icon below to see and discuss what happens to the decimal point when the number is multiplied by 10 or 100. Ask students what would happen if a number were multiplied by 1,000.

Mini-Lesson
1. Work through the ten questions on pages 3 to 14 of the Notebook file. The questions provide practice in multiplying decimals by 10, 100, or 1,000.

2. Ask students to work out their answers on individual whiteboards first, and then to share their answers with a partner.

3. Invite one student to the SMART Board to drag and drop the lily pads into the correct order, directed by the rest of the class. Tell him or her to write the answer in the cloud.

4. Check the answers on each page by moving the frogs at the bottom of the screen.

5. Annotate the place value of the numbers. Encourage students to explain the effects of multiplying by 10, 100, or 1,000.

Independent Work
Give each student two number dice and one multiplier die (see Before You Start). First, ask students to roll one of the number dice to get a number with decimal places. Next, have them roll their multiplier die. Students have to calculate and record the results in a number sentence. For example, if they roll 32.019 and x10, the number sentence is 32.019 x 10 = 320.19.

Wrap-Up
Go to page 15 of the Notebook file and invite students to offer some of the examples they used during Independent Work. Which ones did they find particularly difficult? Invite individuals to write their difficult number sentences on the Notebook page. Suggest that they use the *Moving Digits Interactive Teaching Program* to demonstrate what happens to a number when it is multiplied by 10, 100, or 1,000. Discuss any other difficulties and what methods students used.

Lying Between Decimals

Learning objectives

- Use decimal notation for tenths, hundredths, and thousandths.
- Order decimals with up to three places, and position them on a number line.

Resources

- "Lying Between Decimals" Notebook file
- "Dice Template" (p. 58)
- individual whiteboards and pens, or math notebooks for recording

Whiteboard tools

- Pen tool
- Select tool
- On-screen Keyboard (Select Number pad from the On-screen Keyboard's drop-down menu to type numerals.)

Before You Start

Use the "Dice Template" (p. 58) to create one decimal die for each middle- and higher-ability group, and two dice for lower-ability groups. On each face, write a decimal number, varying the decimals according to ability (for more-confident learners use numbers with up to three decimal places).

Getting Started

Go to page 2 of the "Lying Between Decimals" Notebook file. Encourage students to think about what a decimal is. Write their responses on the Notebook page. Ask students to think about how to find a decimal number that lies between 1.1 and 1.2. Write their responses on the Notebook page. Invite volunteers to come to the SMART Board and add one or two examples of decimals to the number line. Address any difficulties that may have arisen.

Mini-Lesson

1. Look at the number line on page 3 of the Notebook file. Encourage students to write a number on their individual whiteboards that they think will lie between the two given numbers. Invite one student to come to the SMART Board to write his or her response on the number line.

2. Ask students if there are any other numbers that could be used. Invite more volunteers to add their numbers to the number line.

3. Challenge students to name a number between two existing numbers on the number line. Move the numbers along the line to add the new number in the space.

4. Examine the place value of the digits in the various numbers. Ask, for example: *Which is closer to 3.4? Is it 3.45 or 3.451? What about 3.449?*

5. Continue in this manner for the next five number lines on pages 4 to 8.

Independent Work

Divide the class into similar-ability groups. Give each group a decimal die (see Before You Start). Ask students to draw a three-columned table in their notebooks with the headings "Lowest Number," "Middle Number," and "Highest Number." First, ask students to roll the decimal die and to record the number in the "Lowest Number" column of their table. Then have them add 0.1 to this number and record the result in the "Highest Number" column. Next, in the middle column of the table, ask students to write a number that lies in between the two decimal numbers.

Allow less-confident learners to work in pairs. Give them two dice to roll and encourage them to write a decimal number that lies between the two different numbers. Support them in identifying which is the higher and lower number.

Wrap-Up

Encourage students to think of questions from Independent Work where they had difficulties. Work through these questions as a whole group, addressing any misconceptions that students may have. Use page 9 of the Notebook file to make a note of students' responses.

Ordering and Rounding Decimals

Learning objectives
- Use decimal notation for tenths, hundredths, and thousandths.
- Expand, round, and order decimals with up to three places.

Resources
- "Ordering and Rounding Decimals" Notebook file
- individual whiteboards and pens
- index cards

Whiteboard tools
- Pen tray
- Select tool
- Delete button

Before You Start
Prepare sets of cards with decimal numbers for students to order by tenths, hundredths, and thousandths. Numbers should include different tenths (for example, 24.123, 24.234, 24.345) or hundredths (for example, 24.123, 24.134, 24.145). For less-confident learners, prepare sets in which only the tenths are different (such as 24.123, 24.223, 24.323).

Getting Started
Go to page 2 of the "Ordering and Rounding Decimals" Notebook file and ask students to round 23.341 to the nearest tenth. Ask them to write the answer on their individual whiteboards and then hold up the boards to show you. If any students have an incorrect answer, repeat the question and emphasize that you are asking them to round to the nearest tenth. Then delete the blue box on the screen to reveal the answer.

Now ask students how they would round the next number (43.451). At this stage, you may wish to use the Eraser from the Pen tray to reveal the hint: We round up if the number is halfway between two tenths. Round up or down the other numbers on page 2. Invite students to show the answers on their whiteboards before checking the answer on screen. If students continue to struggle, work with them, showing the relative position of the numbers in a simple number line on page 3.

Mini-Lesson
1. Discuss the place value of decimals. Ask: *What makes one decimal number larger than another?*

2. Go to page 4 of the Notebook file. Look at the three numbers and ask students to rearrange them and write them in the correct order on their individual whiteboards. Ask them to hold up their boards when they have finished.

3. Check students' answers, noting any misconceptions. Then use the Eraser from the Pen tray to reveal the correct answer at the bottom of the page.

4. If students struggle to place the numbers in the correct order, highlight the place value of digits in the numbers.

5. Repeat this activity on pages 5 to 10 of the Notebook file.

6. To vary the activity, invite a volunteer to drag the clouds on the Notebook file into the correct number order. Have the other students write *correct* or *incorrect* on their whiteboards and hold them up. Ask a student holding *incorrect* to come to the board to explain why.

Independent Work
Give each group a set of number cards (see Before You Start) and ask students to arrange them in ascending or descending order. Have students swap sets of cards at regular intervals.

Wrap-Up
Discuss any difficulties that may have arisen during Independent Work. Work through these difficulties as a class, encouraging students to think of ways to overcome them. Finish by going to page 11 of the Notebook file to discuss rounding up or down. This will reinforce the work done in the Getting Started activity.

Percentages, Part 1

Learning objective

- Express one quantity as a percentage of another.

Resources

- "Percentages, Part 1" Notebook file
- "Percentage Problems" (p. 60)
- individual whiteboards and pens

Whiteboard tools

- Pen tool
- Select tool

Getting Started

Organize students into mixed-ability groups. Ask them to think about and discuss what a *percentage* is. Add their suggestions to page 2 of the "Percentages, Part 1" Notebook file. If necessary, reveal the definition on the SMART Board (a percentage is the number of parts in every 100) and discuss what it means.

Make a link to your work on number facts to 100 (see "Make 100," p. 13). Identify one number and ask students to write the number needed to make 100 on their individual whiteboards. Repeat for two or three examples and write these on the Notebook page as a prompt.

Mini-Lesson

1. Read out the question on page 3 of the Notebook file. Ask students to vote on the correct percentage by writing the appropriate letter on their individual whiteboards.

2. After they have done this and you have taken a tally of their votes, invite a volunteer to come to the SMART Board and move the apples to reveal the correct answer.

3. Repeat this activity on pages 4 to 9 of the Notebook file.

4. For each question, encourage students to look at how many parts of 100 have been bought, read, and so on, and from this find the correct percentage (or the percentage remaining).

5. If necessary, annotate methods of figuring out answers on the Notebook pages.

6. Make sure all students' answers are recorded on their individual whiteboards. Identify any common misconceptions, ready to discuss during the Independent Work and Wrap-Up.

Independent Work

Give each student a copy of "Percentage Problems" (p. 60). Ask students to work through questions 1 to 8.

Provide support for less-confident learners as they work through questions 1 to 4 initially. Challenge more-confident learners to complete questions 9 to 12 of the worksheet once they have completed the first eight questions. As an additional challenge, ask students to write their own percentage questions for a partner to answer.

Wrap-Up

Invite those students who made up some percentage questions (as an extension to Independent Work) to pose them for the whole class to solve. Write some of students' questions on page 10 of the Notebook file and use them as Getting Started activities in subsequent sessions. Discuss any difficulties that students experienced with the worksheet and highlight any common misconceptions.

Percentages, Part 2

Learning objective
- Find equivalent percentages, decimals, and fractions.

Resources
- "Percentages, Part 2" Notebook file
- "What Percentage?" (p. 61)
- individual whiteboards and pens

Whiteboard tools
- Pen tray
- Select tool

Getting Started
Remind students of previous work done on finding percentages (see p. 24). Together, talk about the link with fractions and work through the example on page 2 of the "Percentages, Part 2" Notebook file: Students need to calculate 50% of 36. Establish that 50% of 36 is the same as $1/2$ of 36, so dividing 36 by 2 will give us 50%.

Show page 3 of the Notebook file. Remind students that a percentage is the number of parts in every 100. Relate this to fractions and the problem on page 2: 50% is the same as $50/100$, which can be simplified to $1/2$. The common factor of $50/100$ is 50.

Ask students to write on their individual whiteboards a list of common factors for given simple numbers such as 12, 15, 100, and so on.

Mini-Lesson
1. Challenge students to work through the questions displayed on pages 4 to 13 of the Notebook file. Each time, ask them to write their answer on their individual whiteboards and then hold up their boards so that you can take a tally of their votes.

2. Encourage students to compare methods of figuring out each answer with a partner.

3. Invite individual students to come to the SMART Board to show their work. Ask if anyone had a different way of finding the answer. If so, invite these students to show the way they worked out the answer.

4. Finally, press the answer options to hear whether or not they are correct. (You will hear a cheer for a correct answer and a groan for an incorrect one.)

Independent Work
Give each student a copy of "What Percentage?" (p. 61). Ask students to work through the questions 1 to 10 initially. These questions contain answers of 10%, 50%, 20%, or 25%.

Limit less-confident learners to questions 1 to 5 initially. These questions contain answers of either 10% or 50%. Challenge more-confident learners to tackle questions 11 to 15 in which the answers are either 40% or 75%. As an additional challenge, ask students to make up their own percentage questions for a partner.

Wrap-Up
Ask students to state what they found difficult, and what methods of finding solutions they used. Make a note of students' comments on page 14 of the Notebook file. Work through any difficulties as a whole class, encouraging contributions from all students.

Solving Word Problems

Learning objectives

- Solve one- and two-step problems involving numbers.
- Choose and carry out appropriate calculations.
- Refine and use efficient written methods to add and subtract two-digit and three-digit whole numbers.

Resources

- "Solving Word Problems" Notebook file
- "Word Problems" (p. 62)

Whiteboard tools

- Pen tray
- Select tool

Getting Started

Display page 2 of the "Solving Word Problems" Notebook file. Read the question out loud and ask students for the answer. Invite them to share their answers and count the legs to check. Repeat this for pages 3 and 4.

Explain that you will now ask a series of simple word problems for students to solve mentally, without pictures. They should state the answer and explain their mental method. Say, for example: *I'm thinking of a number. I add 22 to it, and the answer is 44. What was my number?* Or, *Jodie has 42 colored pens. Kareem has half as many. How many does Kareem have?* Write the answers as number sentences on page 5.

Mini-Lesson

1. Explain to students that they will be solving complex word problems involving multistep operations.

2. Reveal the problem on page 6 of the Notebook file. Ask: *What information does this give us? What do we need to find out? How can we do this?*

3. Ask students how they would complete the first step in the problem. (They will need to add the books on the top and bottom shelves.) Invite them to suggest which method to use. Use a pencil-and-paper method, writing this on the Notebook page.

4. Discuss what the next step should be. (Subtracting the total for the two shelves from the overall total) Again, record this on the SMART Board.

5. Delete the book to check if you are right.

6. Repeat this for the other problems on pages 7 and 8.

Independent Work

Provide each student with a copy of "Word Problems" (p. 62). Ask students to work individually to solve the first problem. They should then compare their method with a partner and discuss which method (if there is a difference) is more appropriate, and why. Have them repeat this for the other three problems on the reproducible sheet.

Decide whether or not to work together as a group with less-confident learners. Demonstrate how to record their thinking on paper or on the SMART Board. Ask students to show their work on their sheets. More-confident learners could invent their own word problem, which should have multiple steps.

Wrap-Up

Review each problem from the reproducible sheet. Invite students from each ability group to explain how they worked out the answer. Ask: *Which method do you think is best? Why do you think that?* Invite one student to show his or her work by writing on page 9 of the Notebook file. Use pages 10 to 13 to check the answers and methods. Invite the more-confident learners to take turns reading out their invented word problems for the others to try to solve.

Superheroes

Learning objective

- Solve one- and two-step problems involving whole numbers and decimals and all four operations, choosing and using appropriate calculation strategies.

Resources

- "Superheroes" Notebook file
- "Superhero Problems" (p. 63)
- individual whiteboards and pens

Whiteboard tools

- Pen tray
- Highlighter pen
- Select tool

Getting Started

Display page 2 of the "Superheroes" Notebook file. Play "Guess My Number": You think of a number and tell students which times table it is in; students ask questions to which you can answer only "yes" or "no." Encourage questions that narrow down the possible answers (*Is it odd or even? Is it less than 20?*). The winner chooses the next number.

Mini-Lesson

1. Go to page 3 of the Notebook file and ask volunteers to read the statements that explain the steps to solving word problems. Have them put the steps into the correct sequence by dragging and dropping them.

2. Read the problem on page 4. Explain that reading the problem is the first step to answering it. Ask: *How should we begin to work this out?*

3. Discuss what math operation is required and ask volunteers to highlight the key math points in the sentence on the SMART Board.

4. Ask: *Is there any information missing?* (The top temperature of an average oven, which is 450°F) Explain to students that they have now completed the second step.

5. Next, students should organize this information onto their individual whiteboards to begin solving the problem in pairs. This is the third step.

6. The fourth step involves completing the problem and answering it. Invite students to explain their solutions to the rest of the class, or to show their work and solutions on the SMART Board.

7. Check these solutions together, explaining that this is the fifth and final step.

8. Try this sequence again with the next problem on page 5 of the Notebook file.

Independent Work

Give out copies of "Superhero Problems" (p. 63). Have students solve the problems using the five-step method. They can choose which problems they want to tackle and in which order to do them.

Less-confident learners could highlight what information is needed to solve the problems on the worksheet and what math strategy is needed to solve them. Encourage more-confident learners to complete the sheet, working through all the problems.

Wrap-Up

Review students' solutions, investigating the math strategies they have used. Make notes on page 6 of the Notebook file. Explain that the problems are challenging because there is so much math involved. Following a simple five-step system helps keep things clear. Go to page 3, which should now show the five steps in the correct order, and ask the class to chant the five steps to math problem paradise! For their homework, invite students to make a list of four of their favorite superheroes for the next lesson.

More Superheroes

Learning objective
- Solve one- and two-step problems involving whole numbers and decimals and all four operations, choosing and using appropriate calculation strategies.

Resources
- "More Superheroes" Notebook file
- "More Superhero Problems" (p. 64)
- individual whiteboards and pens
- calculators

Whiteboard tools
- Pen tray
- On-screen Keyboard
- Select tool
- Highlighter pen

Getting Started
Display page 2 of the "More Superheroes" Notebook file. Establish that 0 is in the middle of the number line. Ask students to draw the same line on their individual whiteboards. Then ask them for three positive and three negative numbers between –20 and +20. Write these numbers randomly on the SMART Board. (Or use the On-screen Keyboard to add numbers to the page.) Ask students to order the six numbers on their number lines. Collect answers and ask for a volunteer to move the numbers in order on the board. Extend the activity by telling students that you have reversed the signs, so negative numbers are now positive and vice versa. Ask a student to reorder the numbers on the board.

Mini-Lesson
1. Review the five steps to solving a problem from the "Superheroes" lesson (p. 27).

2. Display page 3 of the Notebook file and read aloud the problem. Discuss what information the class needs and invite volunteers to highlight the parts of the problem that supply the information.

3. Ask the class to break the problem into two parts and invite students to explain each part. Identify that the first part of the problem is 14 x 8, and that the second part is (14 x 8) x 7. Demonstrate the solution.

4. Look at the problem on page 4. This problem involves different operations. Invite students to highlight the key math parts and ask the class to discuss what different types of operations are being used with this problem (addition and division), and how they could be used together to solve the question.

5. If students need more practice, work through the third example on page 5.

Independent Work
Give out copies of "More Superhero Problems" (p. 64) for students to complete, using the five-step method. All the problems are multisteps. Students can choose which problems they want to do and in which order to do them.

Less-confident learners could highlight what information is needed to solve each problem, and what operation is needed to solve it. Encourage more-confident learners to work through all the problems.

Wrap-Up
Review the solutions from a number of students. Ask them what math strategy they used and make a note of this on page 6 of the Notebook file. Discuss how, with multistep problems, a wider range of math operations is needed to work out the answer.

Numbers and Shapes

Learning objective
- Represent and interpret sequences, patterns, and relationships involving numbers and shapes.

Resources
- "Numbers and Shapes" Notebook file
- "Square and Triangular Numbers Chart" (p. 65)
- individual whiteboards and pens

Whiteboard tools
- Pen tray
- Shapes tool
- Screen Shade
- Highlighter pen
- Select tool

Getting Started

Display page 2 of the "Numbers and Shapes" Notebook file, which shows a rectangle. Draw attention to the side measurement given. Challenge students to figure out, using individual whiteboards, what the other side measurement will be if one side is 8 centimeters and the perimeter is 30 centimeters.

Collect students' answers, then erase the red shapes on the Notebook page to reveal the correct answers. Ask: *What is the area of this rectangle?* Share answers and discuss strategies.

Now consider whether a rectangle with this perimeter could have other dimensions. Collect and record students' suggestions and ask them to work out the areas in their heads.

Repeat the activity, using 42 centimeters for the perimeter. Discuss answers, addressing any misconceptions.

Mini-Lesson

1. Explain that the ancient Greeks represented whole numbers as geometric shapes, often with pebbles on the sand. Go to page 3 of the Notebook file, which shows the standard five Pythagorean number-shapes. Use the Screen Shade to focus on the name and definition of one number-shape at a time.

2. Ask students to discuss the triangular number and its definition. Agree that a triangular number is the number of pebbles in a triangular array.

3. Go to page 4 and explain that the numbers in the chart have been shown up to the third shape. Using the square number, give the next shape (4 x 4) and the next (5 x 5). Repeat with the triangular number, giving the fourth and fifth triangle shapes. Use the Shapes tool (or a Pen from the Pen tray) to show the pattern of triangular numbers.

Independent Work

Provide each student with a copy of "Square and Triangular Numbers Chart" (p. 65). Complete the first row on page 4 of the Notebook file, showing the pattern for the first square and triangular number. Challenge students to find the square and triangular numbers up to the tenth shape and to complete the table on the reproducible page.

Give less-confident learners some counting beads (or similar materials) for support. Work with students at the SMART Board to demonstrate how the pattern builds. Challenge more-confident learners to develop a pattern for rectangular numbers to the tenth number. Display page 5, which shows how the pattern begins. Use the pattern to develop a formula for the twentieth and fiftieth shape in this pattern.

Wrap-Up

Discuss the patterns created and the types of numbers produced. Use the large multiplication grid on page 6 of the Notebook file to show where the numbers fall for square, triangular, and rectangular numbers. Encourage students to look for and explain patterns that appear.

Number Patterns

- Solve multistep problems and problems involving decimals.
- Choose and use appropriate calculation strategies at each stage.

Resources
- "Number Patterns" Notebook file
- individual whiteboards and pens

Whiteboard tools
- Pen tray
- Select tool
- Shapes tool (Use the Shapes tool to demonstrate the pattern of triangular numbers.)

Getting Started

Open the "Number Patterns" Notebook file and go to page 2. Read the number sentence: 7 x 8 = 56. Ask students to state facts that can be derived from this fact. Record their suggestions, for example:

$$56 \div 8 = 7 \qquad\qquad 5.6 \div 8 = 0.7$$

Press the Hint button for further examples. Prompt students to identify, extend, and explain particular patterns of facts. For example: *If you know 7 x 8 = 56, you also know that 56 ÷ 8 = 7.*

Move on to page 3, which shows the number sentence 6 x 9 = 54. Ask students to derive as many related facts as they can in two minutes. Use the on-screen timer to time them (you can start and pause it by pressing the blue button). Collect examples to identify patterns.

Repeat using another multiplication fact, with students recording only division facts.

Mini-Lesson

1. Display page 4 of the Notebook file to remind students about triangular numbers.

2. Use page 5 to demonstrate that if two consecutive triangular numbers are placed together, they produce a square number. For example: 1 + 3 = 4; 3 + 6 = 9. Invite students, in pairs or small groups, to choose any two consecutive triangular numbers to prove this.

3. Ask the class to investigate what happens when a triangular number is doubled. (A rectangular number is created.) Use page 4 to test these rules.

4. Explain that for the remainder of the lesson, the class will be investigating other formulas.

Independent Work

Look at the grid on page 6 of the Notebook file. Explain to students that square numbers can be made up from triangular numbers using two different formulas—the one that the class has already investigated and another, which states that 8 times any triangular number, plus 1, is a square number. Ask students to investigate this in groups by using triangles that are made up of either three or six cubes, plus one. Challenge students to test out the formula with a range of triangular numbers. Compare square numbers and patterns.

Wrap-Up

Ask each group to explain their formula to the class. Have their investigations proven their formula? Make notes on page 7 of the Notebook file. Display the chart on page 8 of the Notebook file. Explain that number shapes extend beyond triangular numbers and square numbers. They can be shown as hexagons, pentagons, octagons, and so on. Tell students that number shapes can have relations with one another (for example, 6 is a triangular and hexagonal number).

Telling Time

- Read time to the nearest minute.
- Use A.M., P.M., and 12-hour clock notation.
- Choose units of time to measure time intervals.
- Calculate time intervals from clocks.

Resources
- "Telling Time" Notebook file
- "How Long?" (p. 66)

Whiteboard tools
- Pen tray
- Select tool

Getting Started

Display page 2 of the "Telling Time" Notebook file. Write a time, in words, at the top of the page, and invite a pair of students to place the hands on the analog clock in the correct place using the Select tool, and write the correct digits into the digital clock. (Press on the end of the clock hands to rotate them.) Use times of five-minute intervals, such as twenty past six, quarter to ten. Invite the other students to check that they agree. Use the Eraser from the Pen tray to delete the writing and invite another pair to try the activity. Repeat for several more pairs.

Mini-Lesson

1. Reveal the pair of clocks on page 3 of the Notebook file. Ask: *What time does the first analog clock show?* Invite a student to write this time on the digital clock. Repeat for the second clock.

2. Repeat this for the clocks on page 4. For the second clock ask: *How many minutes past the hour does the clock show?* Invite students to count the minutes as you point to the minute marks on the clock. Ask: *So what is the time?* Invite a student to write in the time on the digital clock to match.

3. Repeat this for the next pairs of clocks on pages 5 to 8.

4. Look at the pair of clocks on page 9. Read the problem next to the clocks. Encourage students to solve the problem and write the answer in the space provided.

5. Challenge students to make up time word problems for the next two pairs of clocks on page 10, and answer them. This page shows a mixture of analog and digital clocks.

Independent Work

Distribute copies of "How Long?" (p. 66) and ask students to solve the problems, working cooperatively in pairs.

Work with the less-confident learners as a group. Say the time on each clock together, counting the minutes where necessary. Encourage students to suggest a word problem for each. Provide analog and digital clock templates for more-confident learners. Challenge them to use them to write some times and to create word problems to go with them. These can be scanned into the computer for the Wrap-Up. (To upload scanned images, select Insert, then Picture File, and browse to where you have saved the image.)

Wrap-Up

Display the pair of clocks on page 11 of the Notebook file. Ask students to say the difference between the times and suggest a time sentence to go with them. For example, a suitable sentence might be: *The meal started at 12:37 and finished at 1:41, so it lasted for one hour and four minutes.* Repeat this for the pair of clocks on page 12. Invite the more-confident group to reveal one of their scanned-in time word problems for other students to solve. Repeat for the other time word problems.

Movie Times

Learning objective
- Read timetables and time using 24-hour clock notation.

Resources
- "Movie Times" Notebook file
- individual whiteboards and pens
- examples of movie running times (in minutes), from DVDs, videos, or listings (you will need about ten examples)

Whiteboard tools
- Pen tray
- Delete button
- Select tool

Getting Started

Use page 2 of the "Movie Times" Notebook file to practice counting on and back from 0 to 1 in steps of 0.1, from different start points. Annotate the line, using different colors, to illustrate different jump sizes. Point to various places on the line, and ask: *If this is 0.3, what will this be? If we jump in steps of 0.3, which numbers will be in the sequence?* Use the Delete button to remove the circles to reveal the decimal numbers 0.1, 0.2, 0.3, and so on.

Mini-Lesson

1. Display page 3 of the Notebook file. Ask students to help you put the movies in order, from shortest to longest.

2. Ask students how these times have been presented. (In minutes only, for example, 90 minutes)

3. Ask students: *How could we translate these times from minutes to hours and minutes? What do we need to know?*

4. Guide them towards identifying that 1 hour = 60 minutes. Therefore, each number of minutes is a multiple of 60, and whatever is left over are the remaining minutes, or part of one hour.

5. Let students work in pairs to change the movie times into hours and minutes. Have them write the answers on their individual whiteboards. Share results, and check answers.

6. Press the red box to reveal the converted movie times on the next page. To view the two versions together, use the Dual Page Display (select View from the top toolbar, then Zoom, then Dual Page Display).

7. Go to page 5. Work through the examples of movies that you have brought in, converting the lengths from minutes into hours and minutes.

8. Now go to page 6. Tell students to imagine that they are members of a plane's flight crew. Their job is to select movies that will, as near as possible, add up to match the flight time (seven and a half hours).

Independent Work

Working in pairs, have students choose which movies they think will fit the flight time. They can use whatever method they like but it must be linked to time and not preference.

Less-confident learners can add together pairs of times. They can then estimate how many movies the flight attendants could realistically put together for one flight. Challenge more-confident learners to carry out the activity for different flight lengths.

Wrap-Up

Ask the class if anybody got near to the flight time. Using page 7 of the Notebook file, ask different pairs to write up which movies they chose and how they got to their answer. Discuss other reasons for choosing movies. For example, trying to show the maximum number of movies in one flight might not be a good idea, as longer movies may be more absorbing and make the flight seem shorter.

Ratio Problems

Learning objective

- Solve simple problems involving direct proportion by scaling quantities up or down.

Resources

- "Ratio Problems" Notebook file
- tape measure
- calculators
- paper and pens

Whiteboard tools

- Pen tray
- Select tool
- Highlighter pen
- Delete button

Getting Started

Open page 2 of the "Ratio Problems" Notebook file. Explain that a number of colored lollipops have been put into the box: one yellow, four red, three green, and two blue lollipops. Highlight key vocabulary: *unlikely, equal, likely, certain chance.* Ask: *If you were to pick a lollipop from the box, what is the most likely color to be picked?* Agree that it is red. Drag one out of the box and see.

Ask students to make statements about the probability of selecting the color of lollipops, using the words on the Notebook file. What other words or phrases might be added to the list? Ensure that *equally likely, even chance,* and *some* are added. With each word or phrase, encourage students to make a statement about the lollipops in the container.

Add or remove lollipops from the box at intervals to change the probability. Ask: *How many lollipops should we add to the box so that picking each color is equally likely?* Ensure that students understand the idea of equally likely outcomes.

Mini-Lesson

1. Explain to students that they are going to investigate proportion. Where would they use the word *proportion*? Collect answers, ascertaining that proportion is relative to an object's real size. Reveal the definition on page 3 of the Notebook file.

2. Explain that you will be looking at the relationship between normal cars and model cars and that this is expressed as a *ratio*.

3. Go to page 4. Explain that the ratio of the model car is 1:20, meaning the car is $1/20$ of the size of the original.

4. Draw students' attention to the equation for working out the original size: 12.5cm x 20 = 250cm.

5. Encourage students to discuss if they think this is accurate.

6. Ask what would happen if the model car was 8cm long. Explain that to increase the ratio size, the number after the colon increases (so it would be 1:8). Compare and investigate the ratios 1:10 and 1:30. Can students tell you which would be a realistic car size? Use a meter stick to demonstrate the agreed-upon length.

Independent Work

Show the class the six different ratios and the cars with their sizes indicated on page 5 of the Notebook file. Explain that the toy company has mixed up the ratios and has asked you to pair up cars with correct ratios. In mixed-ability groups, ask students to work out the answers on paper. Then invite representatives from each group to come to the SMART Board to drag and drop one ratio alongside a car. After they have done this, press the arrow to check the answers provided on page 6.

Wrap-Up

Share lists and discuss any disagreements. Ask the group representatives to show their work on pages 7 and 8 of the Notebook file. Agree that the larger the original object is, the larger the ratio is likely to be. Explain that the ratio can be found by dividing the size of the model by the original size of the object. Set the Wrap-Up activity on page 9 as homework.

Measuring

Learning objective

- Interpret intervals and divisions on partially numbered scales and record readings accurately, where appropriate to the nearest tenth of a unit.

Resources

- "Measuring" Notebook file
- "Reading Scales" (p. 67)

Whiteboard tools

- Pen tray
- Select tool
- Lines tool

Getting Started

Display page 2 of the "Measuring" Notebook file. Ask students to look at the first ruler and to say what measurement they see on it. (cm) Discuss the scale, and how it is marked. Ask students to read the measurements. Repeat this for the other rulers, ensuring that students understand that for some of the rulers, they will need to estimate how many millimeters there are between the markings.

Mini-Lesson

1. Display page 3 of the Notebook file and discuss the scale on the ruler, noting that the markings between each centimeter are in millimeters.

2. Invite students to make estimates of the readings and then to look carefully to check the readings. Encourage them to do this accurately. Discuss whether to round up or down to the nearest half centimeter, and why this may be appropriate. Check that students understand that millimeters can be expressed as a decimal fraction of a centimeter.

3. Display page 4 and discuss how the containers are marked, and how to read the scale.

4. Ask students to read the water levels, and to make estimates where necessary. Encourage them to explain their estimates.

5. Go to page 5. Again, discuss the scale and invite students to estimate the readings. Repeat this for page 6.

6. Display page 7, which shows three lines. Invite a student to move the ruler until it lines up with the first line. Discuss how to make the measurement to the nearest half centimeter. Repeat for the other two lines.

Independent Work

Give each student a copy of "Reading Scales" (p. 67) to complete. As students work, discuss how they make their estimates, and how accurate they think these are.

Less-confident learners could be asked to read to the nearest cm, nearest 100ml, and nearest 10kg. Challenge more-confident learners to read to the nearest mm, nearest 25ml, and nearest 5kg.

When students have completed the sheet, ask them to use a ruler to draw some lines on the back of the sheet. Have them work with a partner to measure the lines to the nearest half centimeter.

Wrap-Up

With students watching, draw some thick lines on page 8 of the Notebook file using the Lines tool. Have individuals take turns moving the ruler into place so that it lines up with the drawn line. Invite students to read, from the ruler, the length of the line to the nearest half centimeter. They could try using a real ruler as well, to check that the measurements are the same. Ask students: *How do you decide whether to round a measurement up or down?*

Metric Units of Measurement

Learning objective

- Select and use metric units of measure and convert between units using decimals to two places (e.g., change 2.75 liters to 2,750ml, or vice versa).

Resources

- "Metric Units of Measurement" Notebook file
- "Standard Metric Units" (p. 68)
- a range of objects to measure length, mass, and capacity (such as lengths of rope, packages, nonstandard containers filled with water)
- measuring tools
- individual whiteboards and pens
- writing materials

Whiteboard tools

- Pen tray
- Fill Color tool
- Select tool
- Delete button

Getting Started

Encourage students to work in mixed-ability groups. Provide them with paper and pens and invite them to think of the different metric units of measurement for length, mass, and capacity, with their abbreviations.

Come back together as a whole class. Using the Fill Color tool, reveal the units for length, mass, and capacity by selecting a dark color to fill the first column of the tables on pages 2 and 3 of the "Metric Units of Measurement" Notebook file. Repeat in the second column to reveal each of the abbreviations.

Ask students to think about the relationships between the units of measurement for length, for example. Encourage them to suggest equivalent values by asking questions such as: *How many millimeters make a centimeter?* Fill the third column of each table to reveal a selection of equivalent values.

Mini-Lesson

1. Go to page 4 of the Notebook file and ask students: *What is the metric unit for temperature? What is its abbreviation?* Encourage students to record their answers on their individual whiteboards before revealing the answers on the screen. If appropriate, ask them if they know at what temperature water boils. Again, encourage students to record their responses before revealing the answer.

2. Go to page 5 of the Notebook file and press the images to open the Interactive Teaching Programs. Explore mass, capacity, temperature, and length in turn. (Press on the *i* icon for information on how to work each program.)

3. Set different measures and scales using the buttons on the screen. Ask students to identify each measure and scale, and to predict the effect of adding or subtracting mass, volume, and so on. Experiment with different scales.

4. Encourage students to work in pairs in order to check answers.

5. Model the range of measuring tools available for students to use during Independent Work. Leave the completed unit and abbreviation charts on the SMART Board for reference.

Independent Work

Set up a group of tables with one table for each of the following:

- measuring length using rulers, tape measures, and meter sticks
- measuring mass using kitchen and bathroom scales
- measuring capacity using measuring cups

Using their copies of "Standard Metric Units" (p. 68), ask students to explore the range of equipment set out on the tables. They should write down the object to be measured, the unit to measure it in, and the actual measurement. Rotate the groups around the tables, with each group spending about ten minutes per table.

Wrap-Up

Work through any misconceptions and difficulties that students may have had, or that you have observed. If time is available, work through pages 6 to 19 of the Notebook file to assess students' understanding.

Suitable Units of Measurement

Learning objectives
- Select and use metric units of measure.
- Read and interpret scales on a range of measuring tools.

Resources
- "Suitable Units of Measurement" Notebook file
- "Measuring Things" (p. 69)
- individual whiteboards and pens
- measuring tools such as rulers and tapes (length), scales and balances (weight), measuring cups and cylinders (capacity)
- a selection of small items to measure

Whiteboard tools
- Pen tray
- Select tool
- Delete button

Getting Started
Go to page 2 of the "Suitable Units of Measurement" Notebook file and match the appropriate tool to the object to be measured—for example, the measuring cup or thermometer can be used for the milk bottle. Invite volunteers to come to the SMART Board to drag and drop the labels into position next to the matching images. Encourage students to give clear reasons for each of their choices.

Discuss the importance of using the correct tools for measuring. Prompt students to consider what would happen if the correct tool was not used. Ask: *What would you use to measure the weight of a paper clip? Could you use bathroom scales? What would you use to measure the thickness of a paper clip? Could you use a ruler with no markings for millimeters?*

Mini-Lesson
1. Remind students about the work in the previous lesson on "Metric Units of Measurement" (p. 35). Explore the terms *length*, *weight* (or *mass*), and *capacity*.

2. Go to page 3 of the Notebook file. Using their individual whiteboards, ask students to write a list of suitable units of measurement for length. Invite them to tell you their ideas (including U.S. customary measures), then use the Delete button to remove the green box to reveal the units of measurement as they are identified. Repeat for weight and capacity on pages 4 and 5.

3. Revisit pages 3 to 5, this time asking for ideas on the tools needed to carry out measurements accurately for each measure. Circle the correct items as students tell you their ideas.

4. Introduce the different objects arranged on tables (see Resources). Pose the questions: *What measuring tools are available? What would you use each tool to measure?*

5. Challenge students to sort the objects into three groups—length, weight, and capacity—and place each group on its own table.

Independent Work
Have students work in pairs and give each pair time to access the length, weight, and capacity tables (see above). Ask them to make notes on their copy of "Measuring Things" (p. 69), noting object, estimate, and measurement.

Support less-confident learners by allowing them to access the words on pages 3 to 5 of the Notebook file. Challenge the more-confident pairs to measure the objects again, this time using customary measures, if appropriate.

Wrap-Up
Encourage students to give feedback on their findings on page 6 of the Notebook file. Write this feedback onto the prepared grid and prompt for any alternative measurements or tools used. Address any common misconceptions and review the full range of measures and tools used.

Customary Units of Measurement

Learning objectives

- Measure and calculate using customary units.
- Know the approximate metric equivalents of customary units.

Resources

- "Customary Units of Measurement" Notebook file
- tools for some practical measuring activities (see Independent Work)
- construction paper
- pens

Whiteboard tools

- Pen tray
- Select tool

Getting Started

Challenge students to name some customary units of measurement. Write their suggestions on page 2 of the Notebook file. Ask: *How are customary units different from metric units?*

Mini-Lesson

1. Organize students into mixed-ability groups and have them work through the activities on pages 3 to 6 of the Notebook file. On each page is a list of customary and metric measurements. Provide four pieces of construction paper for each group and ask each group to draw a line down the center of each piece of paper, marking one half "Customary" and one half "Metric."

2. Challenge students to work through the words on the list on each page and write them in the appropriate columns. Ask them to mark one another's work by swapping with another group. Discuss and agree on the correct answers.

3. Invite volunteers to come and drag the words into the correct columns on the Notebook pages.

4. Ask if anyone knows the equivalence between any customary and metric units. If necessary, inform students that a mile is about 1,600 meters, 2.2 pounds is one kilogram, and a gallon is around 4.5 liters.

5. Use pages 7 to 9 to establish the equivalent values for metric and customary units. Ask questions, such as: *If one inch is about 2.54 centimeters, how many centimeters is two inches?*

6. Point out that the numbers are not exact and have been rounded up to two decimal places. Pose the problem: *One pint is approximately equal to 568 milliliters and 5.68 liters. How would you round up the liter measurement to one decimal place?*

Independent Work

Organize a center of practical measuring activities. These activities should include measuring using feet and inches; yards; pounds and ounces; pints and gallons. Give students equal time on each activity to measure using customary measurements. Set them to work in mixed-ability groups with support as and where needed.

Wrap-Up

Invite students to share their thoughts on the measuring activities. Do they prefer to measure in metric or customary units, or does it not make a difference? Discuss the advantages and disadvantages of measuring with customary versus metric units. For example, converting inches to feet and inches may be more difficult because it's not a simple case of dividing by 100 (as you would when converting centimeters to meters). Use pages 10 and 11 to assess students' understanding of customary units and to assess whether they can choose suitable units for a particular task. Encourage them to give reasons for their answers. Use page 12 to make notes on what students have learned during this lesson.

Crazy Quads

Learning objective
- Use the formula for the area of a rectangle to calculate its area.

Resources
- "Crazy Quads" Notebook file
- "Quads" (p. 70)
- individual whiteboards and pens
- graph paper (for less-confident learners)

Whiteboard tools
- Pen tray
- Select tool
- Lines tool

Getting Started
Open the "Crazy Quads" Notebook file and go to page 2. Ask the class to discuss how they would find the area of the quadrilateral. Explain that it has to be measured accurately and that in this case they will be using centimeters.

Mini-Lesson
1. Demonstrate how to measure the shape on page 2 of the Notebook file using the on-screen ruler (one square on the grid represents 1cm). Note the lengths of each side on the board. To find the area, use a formula: multiply length by width (L x W = A) (7cm x 5cm = 35cm^2).

2. Point out that area is given in centimeters squared, which is shown using the squared symbol (^{2}).

3. Go to page 3 and choose one of the shapes. Repeat the process using the formula. Then ask a volunteer to count up the squares to show that the number of squares in the quadrilateral is the same as the answer from using the formula.

4. Repeat the activity for the other quadrilaterals.

Independent Work
Give each student a copy of "Quads" (p. 70). Have them measure the quadrilaterals and use the formula to find the areas in centimeters squared.

Less-confident learners could draw the shapes onto graph paper first. Extend the activity for more-confident learners by asking them to cut out two quads and group them to create a new shape. What is the total surface area of this new shape?

Wrap-Up
Ask students to show their work on the SMART Board. Display page 4 of the Notebook file. Ask: *How would you measure the area of these shapes?* Use the Lines tool to cut one of the new shapes into two, creating two quadrilaterals. Measure both these parts of the shape and then add the two areas together for the final total. Repeat for the second shape. Explain that if the quadrilateral is square, the formula that could be used is x^2 (x being the length of one side). The result will therefore be a square number.

Polygon Puzzles

Learning objectives

- Measure and calculate the perimeter of regular and irregular polygons.
- Use the formula for the area of a rectangle to calculate its area.

Resources

- "Polygon Puzzles" Notebook file
- "Quads" (p. 70)
- centimeter rulers

Whiteboard tools

- Pen tray
- Select tool
- Lines tool

Getting Started

Ask students: *What does* perimeter *mean?* (The measurement of the outside edge of a shape or polygon) Go to page 2 of the "Polygon Puzzles" Notebook file and discuss how to measure these shapes. Using the on-screen ruler, measure the shape in centimeters, writing the measurements next to each edge (one square on the grid represents 1cm). Add the measurements together to calculate the perimeter. Explain that perimeter is measured in centimeters, not centimeters squared, like area.

Mini-Lesson

1. Go to page 3 of the Notebook file and ask students to measure the perimeter of the shapes on the page.

2. Display page 4. Explain that each of these new shapes has been made with two quadrilaterals. Although the original quadrilaterals had parallel edges that were the same length, this is no longer the case. Use the Lines tool to show the divisions. Show students how to measure each edge, and point out that the sum of these edges is the perimeter.

3. Use the six squares on page 5 to make different shapes. Show that the perimeter of each new shape can be greater or smaller, even though you are using the same number of blocks.

Independent Work

Give each student a copy of "Quads" (p. 70) to cut out quadrilaterals and create irregular polygons. Have students measure the shapes to find the perimeter, using centimeter rulers.

Less-confident learners could measure the perimeter of the quads on the sheet, rather than cutting them out and rearranging them. (Turn back to page 4 of the Notebook file if this is helpful.) More-confident learners could choose three shapes from the sheet and investigate how the perimeter of a shape changes depending on how the three shapes are combined. Ask: *What are the largest and smallest perimeters possible?*

Wrap-Up

Invite students to show and discuss their work. Students in the more-confident group can show their work about longest and shortest perimeters using the same three shapes. Use page 5 of the Notebook file to demonstrate that because all the sides are the same length, it is possible to count the number of squares to figure out the perimeter. Discuss why this would be important for architects and builders working on a site. Discuss the difference between area and perimeter—that the area can be the same but the perimeter alters. Show this with the six blocks again.

Perimeter Challenge

- Calculate the perimeter and area of rectilinear shapes.
- Estimate the area of an irregular shape by counting squares.

Resources

- "Perimeter Challenge" Notebook file
- graph paper (centimeter-squared)
- individual whiteboards and pens

Whiteboard tools

- Pen tray
- Select tool
- Delete button

Getting Started

Display page 2 of the "Perimeter Challenge" Notebook file. Ask students to recite the 4, 6, and 8 times tables. Repeat for the 40, 60, and 80 times tables and for the 0.4, 0.6, and 0.8 times tables. Delete the panels to display the times tables. Reveal the answers by using the Eraser from the Pen tray. Remind students how these tables are related.

Mini-Lesson

1. Show the rectangle on page 3 of the Notebook file. Review the formulas used to find the area and perimeter of a rectangle or square. Move the rectangle to review the correct formulas:

    Perimeter = (length + width) x 2   Area = length x width

2. Point out the use of parentheses in the first formula. The parentheses indicate that the length and width are added together before the result is multiplied by 2. Ask: *What would happen if the parentheses were removed?*

3. Tell students that they will be creating several compound shapes using rectangles of equal size but that each compound shape must be different from any other.

4. Go to page 4 and explain that these shapes will represent the plans for a new Gnome Ville Housing Estate. Ask students to present their most original ideas. The second diagram on the page shows what happens when two rectangles are combined.

5. Ask the class to consider the effect on the area and perimeter if two rectangles of the same dimensions are joined together. Note that the area doubles (since the rectangles have the same dimensions) but the perimeter does not. Discuss why the perimeter does not double in size.

6. Calculate the area and perimeter of the shape on page 5, annotating as necessary.

7. Erase any calculations, rearrange the shape by selecting and rotating the individual components and labels, and calculate its area and perimeter.

Independent Work

Ask students to create compound Gnome Houses using two or three rectangles of equal size on graph paper.

Wrap-Up

Review the houses created. Invite some students to demonstrate their designs on the SMART Board using the prepared grid and rectangles on page 6 of the Notebook file. Discuss any difficulties they may have experienced. Go back to page 4 to reexamine the second house, pointing out that some measurements are missing for this shape. Discuss how these missing measurements could be calculated from the given information (opposing sides would be the same length, parts of short lengths could be used to subtract from known sides, and so on).

Polygons

Learning objective
- Draw polygons and classify them by identifying their properties, including their line of symmetry.

Resources
- "Polygons" Notebook file
- "Shape Tiles" (p. 71), enlarged, if desired
- scissors
- plastic shape tiles
- paper
- glue

Whiteboard tools
- Pen tray
- Shapes tool
- Select tool
- Lines tool

Getting Started

Open the "Polygons" Notebook file and go to page 2. Describe a polygon for students to guess; for example, *I am thinking of a shape that is regular. It has four right angles.* (Square) Use the Shapes tool to place the shape on the page, so that students can see if they were right. Encourage them to check the shape against your description. Repeat for different polygons.

Mini-Lesson

1. Display page 3 of the Notebook file. Discuss the definition of a *polygon*—a closed, flat shape with three or more straight sides.

2. Discuss the definition of a *regular polygon*—a closed, flat shape with three or more straight sides, and all sides and angles equal.

3. Go to page 4 and tell students you want them to sort the shapes. Point out the title of the table, Sorting Polygons, and the various headings: Triangles, Quadrilaterals, Regular, Not Regular.

4. Ask students to suggest how to sort the shapes and to explain why each shape belongs in its specific place. Invite a volunteer to drag the shapes into the table as they are discussed.

5. Point out the shapes that do not fit into the table. Ask students to explain why they don't belong anywhere. Emphasize that the remaining shapes are neither triangles nor quadrilaterals because they have more than four sides; however, they are all polygons.

6. Use page 5 to discuss the definitions for *equilateral* (all sides and angles equal), *isosceles* (two sides and angles equal), and *right* (one right angle) triangles.

7. Complete the polygon sorting activities on pages 6 and 7. Use the on-screen ruler, if necessary, to measure the sides of the shapes.

Independent Work

Give each student a copy of "Shape Tiles" (p. 71). Ask them to cut out the sets of triangles and to sort them into isosceles, equilateral, and right triangles. They should then use the sets to make patterns. The shape tiles in their patterns must touch, leaving no gaps (tessellation). When students have produced patterns they are happy with, have them glue them onto paper.

Decide whether less-confident learners should use plastic shape tiles and work as a group. Encourage students to describe the properties of the shapes. Provide more-confident learners with some assorted shape tiles. Which shapes tessellate and which do not?

Wrap-Up

Review the patterns that students have made. Discuss the properties of the shapes. Ask questions such as: *Are these shapes polygons? Regular polygons? Is a circle a polygon? Why not?* Record students' observations on page 8 of the Notebook file. Invite the more-confident learners to explain which of the tiles they have been given will tessellate, and to explain why this is so.

Reflections

Learning objective

- Draw polygons and classify them by identifying their properties, including their line of symmetry.

Resources

- "Reflections" Notebook file
- "Reflecting Shapes" (p. 72)
- graph paper (centimeter-squared)
- rulers
- safety mirrors

Whiteboard tools

- Pen tray
- Lines tool
- Gallery

Getting Started

Explain that you will be asking students to draw the reflection of an image. Display page 2 of the "Reflections" Notebook file. Discuss what a reflection is and how you would draw one. Ask students to draw the image on page 2 on graph paper, using the lines to help, and to put in the "mirror line." Invite individual students to describe lines of the image using vocabulary such as *horizontal* and *vertical*. Then ask students to draw the reflection of the image on their graph paper. Ask them to show you this, then invite them to explain how the reflection is the same as, and different from, the original image. Invite individuals to come up and use the Lines tool to draw the reflective image on the Notebook page.

Drag the arrow to check the answer. This will reveal the reflected image of the shape, which could be dragged to the correct place. Repeat for the next shape on page 3 of the Notebook file, checking the reflected image in the same way.

Mini-Lesson

1. Go to page 4 of the Notebook file. Invite students to copy the image on graph paper and then to sketch its reflection.

2. Ask individuals to come up and draw the reflection on the SMART Board. Drag the arrow to reveal the correct reflection.

3. Use the squares on the grid or the ruler from the Gallery to compare the distances between the mirror line and points on the image, and the mirror line and the reflected points. Encourage students to do the same with their rulers.

4. Discuss how equivalent points on the image and its reflection are the same distance from the mirror, or line of symmetry.

5. Repeat for the next images on pages 5, 6, and 7.

Independent Work

Provide each student with a copy of "Reflecting Shapes" (p. 72), a ruler, and a safety mirror. Ask students to complete the sheet individually, but tell them that they can compare and discuss what they are doing with a partner.

Decide whether or not to bring less-confident learners together as a group and to discuss what they see on the sheet. Encourage them to use the vocabulary of symmetry as they describe shapes and lines. Challenge more-confident learners to work in pairs. Using graph paper, have them draw an image of their own, then swap sheets and draw the reflection of their partner's image.

Wrap-Up

Invite individuals to come up and draw their images on page 8 of the Notebook file. Ask another student to draw the reflected image. Clear the page using the Eraser, or press Edit and then Clear Page. Repeat this several times.

Mirror Shapes

Learning objective
- Complete patterns with up to two lines of symmetry.

Resources
- "Mirror Shapes" Notebook file
- "Polygon Shapes" (p. 73)
- individual whiteboards and pens
- small plastic mirrors, one for each student
- large mirror

Whiteboard tools
- Pen tray
- Select tool
- Lines tool

Getting Started
Display page 2 of the "Mirror Shapes" Notebook file. Ask the class to discuss, in pairs, what properties the shape has (corner, side, parallel sides, and so on). Label these properties on the SMART Board.

Mini-Lesson
1. Explain to students that in this lesson they will be looking at another property that many polygons have: symmetry. In pairs, ask students to come up with a definition for *symmetry*. Invite them to explain their definitions and write them on page 3 of the Notebook file. As a class, they should agree on the most correct definition.

2. Go back to page 2 and explain that this rectangle has two lines of reflective symmetry. Use the Lines tool to draw the lines of symmetry on the shape. Use a large mirror to show the lines of symmetry.

3. Display page 4 and ask the class to discuss where they think the lines of symmetry will appear on the first shape. Ask for a volunteer to draw these lines in, and then check them with the mirror. Repeat this with the other polygons. (The shapes can be rotated, if required.)

Independent Work
Give out copies of "Polygon Shapes" (p. 73) and plastic mirrors. Ask students to explore the symmetry of each of the regular shapes, writing beneath each how many lines of symmetry it has (an equilateral triangle has three lines of symmetry, for example).

Wrap-Up
Display page 5 of the Notebook file, which includes the same shapes as on the reproducible sheet. Review the work done by students by asking for volunteers to draw the common lines of symmetry onto the shapes on the SMART Board. Ask students if there were any shapes that they found unusual. Direct the conversation toward circles, which have an infinite number of lines of symmetry. Illustrate this, using page 6 of the Notebook file. Return to the class definition and ask if it needs editing. Make any suggested changes.

Rotation

Learning objective

- Visualize and draw where a shape will be after rotation through 90° or 180° about its center or one of its vertices.

Resources

- "Rotation" Notebook file
- "Rotating Shapes" (p. 74)
- individual whiteboards and pens

Whiteboard tools

- Pen tray
- Select tool
- Shapes tool
- Lines tool

Getting Started

Explain that the purpose of the lesson is to investigate rotating simple shapes through 90°. Discuss the meaning of the word *rotate* and write any definitions on page 2 of the "Rotation" Notebook file. If necessary, pull the arrow to reveal the prepared definition for *rotation*.

Invite students to demonstrate rotation using the shape on page 3. Ask the class to say stop when the shape has been rotated through 90°. Ensure that students understand the words *clockwise* and *counterclockwise* to further describe the rotation.

Mini-Lesson

1. Show students the starting shape on page 4. Explain that you would like them to correctly identify the shape that has been rotated through 90° clockwise. They can do this either by drawing the rotated shapes on their individual whiteboards or by voting for the correct answer by writing *a* or *b* on their boards.

2. Once students have all given an answer, press the most popular selection on the screen. You will hear either a cheer for a correct answer or a groan for an incorrect one.

3. Discuss what the shape would look like if it had been rotated:

   - another 90°

     - in the opposite direction

4. Repeat for the examples on pages 5 to 8.

Independent Work

Give each student a copy of "Rotating Shapes" (p. 74). Ask all students to draw the rotation of the first two shapes. Next, ask students to find shapes around the classroom (or on the SMART Board). Challenge them to draw them in the boxes provided and then to draw their rotation through 90°. Can they draw the rotations through 90° clockwise and counterclockwise?

Support less-confident learners with the first two shapes and, if necessary, demonstrate the rotation of these shapes on the SMART Board. Challenge more-confident learners to find more complex 2D shapes to rotate. Are they able to rotate the shapes by 180°?

Wrap-Up

Review the Independent Work activity with the whole class and focus on the shapes that students drew. Invite one or two students to come to the SMART Board to draw their shapes and their rotations on page 9 of the Notebook file. They may find the Shapes tool or the Lines tool helpful when doing this. Consolidate the work on rotation by asking individual students to come to the board to rotate one of the four shapes on page 10 through 90° (clockwise or counterclockwise). Encourage the whole class to vote on which direction the rotation took.

Identifying Angles

Learning objectives
- Know that angles are measured in degrees and that one whole turn is 360°.
- Draw, compare, and order angles less than 180°.

Resources
- "Identifying Angles" Notebook file
- "What's the Angle?" (p. 75)
- 45° and 60° triangles, one of each for each pair of students

Whiteboard tools
- Pen tray
- Select tool
- Lines tool
- Gallery (Search for "interactive protractor" and drag it to any Notebook page)

Getting Started
Display page 2 of the "Identifying Angles" Notebook file. Ask students to stand up and face the front of the classroom. Explain that you will say an angle and would like them to turn in the direction that you say. Say, for example:

Turn a right angle to the right. Turn two right angles to the right. Now turn another right angle to the right. How many right angles have you turned? And where have you finished? So how many right angles are there if you turn through a complete circle?

Repeat with left, and more right, turns, and using 30°and 60°, as well as 90°.

Mini-Lesson
1. Display page 3 of the Notebook file. Ask students to look carefully at the angles and to say their size. Agree and check with the interactive protractor from the Gallery that these are all 90° angles.

2. Go to page 4 and explain that two different types of angles are shown. Ask for volunteers to use the interactive protractor to measure the angles on the page.

3. Demonstrate how to record and read the angles in degrees.

4. Now display page 5 and ask students to decide which is the smallest angle, the next smallest, and so on. Drag and drop the angles into order from smallest to largest. Use the interactive protractor, if necessary, to measure the angles.

Independent Work
Ask students to work in pairs. Provide each pair with 45° and 60° triangles and a copy of "What's the Angle" (p. 75). Ask each pair to complete the reproducible page.

Decide whether or not to work with less-confident learners as a group, with an 11" x 17" enlargement of the reproducible sheet and the triangles. If more-confident learners complete the work quickly, suggest that they use the triangles to construct some triangles with angles of 45° and 60°.

Wrap-Up
Use page 6 of the Notebook file to draw an angle, using either a Pen from the Pen tray or the Lines tool. Ask students whether the angle you have drawn is larger or smaller than a right angle. Repeat this for other angles, comparing them with 45° and 60° and using the interactive protractor to check.

Acute and Obtuse Angles

Learning objective
- Use a protractor to measure and draw angles.

Resources
- "Acute and Obtuse Angles" Notebook file
- "Acute or Obtuse?" (p. 76)
- protractors
- pencils
- rulers

Whiteboard tools
- Pen tray
- Select tool

Getting Started
Show students the angle on page 2 of the "Acute and Obtuse Angles" Notebook file. Ask them whether they think it is an acute or obtuse angle. Encourage individual students to provide definitions of each type of angle. Prompt them if necessary, pulling out the prepared definitions on the Notebook file. Establish with the whole class that the angle on page 2 is obtuse. Ask: *How could we prove this is an obtuse angle?* Introduce the interactive protractor on the SMART Board and ensure that students know how to use it. (Click and drag on the green dot and align it with one side of the angle. Click on the arrow in the middle of the protractor to switch the side from which to measure.)

Mini-Lesson
1. Work through the angles on pages 3 to 7 of the Notebook file together. Challenge students to make an educated guess as to whether each angle is acute or obtuse.

2. Invite individual students to come to the SMART Board to check each angle using the interactive protractor. Rotate the angle, if required, by selecting it and dragging the green dot.

3. Write the measurement in the space provided at the top of each page.

Independent Work
Give each student a copy of "Acute or Obtuse?" (p. 76). Encourage students to use protractors to draw the angles as given on the sheet and to state whether they are acute or obtuse. On the back of their worksheets, ask students to use the protractor to draw three acute and three obtuse angles, giving the measurement of the angles to the nearest degree.

Support less-confident learners in their use of the protractor to measure and draw. If appropriate, challenge more-confident learners to draw and measure *reflex angles*—angles that measure more than 180°.

Wrap-Up
Share the results of the measuring activities with the whole class. Congratulate students on their successes and discuss any points for development. Use page 8 of the Notebook file to address any difficulties and, if necessary, review the process of drawing and measuring angles using the interactive protractor on the SMART Board.

The Sum of Angles

Learning objectives

- Use a protractor to measure angles, on their own and in shapes.
- Calculate angles in a triangle.

Resources

- "The Sum of Angles" Notebook file
- individual white-boards and pens
- different-shaped triangles made from construction paper or cardboard
- supply of thick paper or cardboard
- protractors

Whiteboard tools

- Pen tray
- Select tool
- Shapes tool
- Lines tool
- Gallery (Search for "interactive protractor" to use in the Getting Started activity.)

Getting Started

Show students the question on page 2 of "The Sum of Angles" Notebook file. Ask: *What is a 90° angle called?* (Right angle) Remind students that a straight line is made up of two right angles.

Reveal the isosceles triangle beneath the red rectangle. Look at the diagram on the right-hand side to illustrate how the angles add up to 180°. Use the interactive protractor found in the Gallery to verify how the angles add up to 180°. Provide a selection of different-shaped triangles and protractors and allow students some time to explore them. Ask: *Do the angles in all the triangles add up to 180°?*

Mini-Lesson

1. Go to page 3 of the Notebook file. Invite students, in pairs, to work out the missing angle. Ask them to write the answer on their individual whiteboards and display them when you say *Show me*.

2. Check the angle using the interactive protractor, which can be resized by selecting it and dragging the white dot, or rotated by selecting it and dragging the green dot.

3. Move the magnifying glass over point *c* to reveal the answer.

4. Work through the other exercises on finding missing angles on pages 4 to 9 in the same way.

Independent Work

Ask students, in pairs, to make their own large triangles from thick paper or cardboard. Challenge them to measure each angle using a protractor.

Give less-confident learners plenty of practice in using the protractor and, if necessary, work with them on the calculations required to find the angles of a triangle. For example, if two of the angles in a triangle are 100° and 50°, the third angle will be 180° – 150° = 30°. Challenge more-confident learners to experiment with a range of different triangles to prove that the same result is always produced. For a further challenge, ask students to investigate whether the four angles in a quadrilateral always add up to 360°.

Wrap-Up

Encourage students to share their work with the class. They could use the Shapes tool or Lines tool to demonstrate their own triangles on the SMART Board. Address any common misconceptions about angles in a triangle or difficulties in measuring angles using a protractor, and write these on page 10 of the Notebook file.

The Truth About Triangles

Learning objective
- Identify, visualize, and describe properties of triangles.

Resources
- "The Truth About Triangles" Notebook file
- "Triangles" (p. 77)
- individual whiteboards and pens
- mirrors

Whiteboard tools
- Pen tray
- Screen Shade
- Lines tool
- Select tool
- On-screen Keyboard

Getting Started

Go to page 2 of the "Truth About Triangles" Notebook file, showing just the first row of numbers: 2, 4, 8, 16, 32, 64. Discuss what is happening in the number sequence. (The numbers are doubling.) Now move the Screen Shade to reveal the second line. Ask for the relationship in this sequence. (They are squared numbers.) Finally, reveal the third line and ask for the relationship. (They are triangular numbers.) Draw the numbers on the board in the shape of a triangle to show this. For example:

$$1$$
$$1 + 2$$
$$1 + 2 + 3$$
$$1 + 2 + 3 + 4$$

Mini-Lesson

1. Go to page 3 of the Notebook file and read the question at the top of the page. Tell students that they will be investigating the properties of different types of triangles and their lines of symmetry.

2. Discuss with students the names of different types of triangles. Write a separate "definition" text box for each type of triangle, listing its name, the number of equal sides, and the number of equal angles. (Simple definitions can be accessed by pulling out the Definitions tab.)

3. Drag triangles out of the box at the bottom of the page. Ask: *Which definition goes with which triangle?* Invite volunteers to match them.

4. Look at pages 4 and 5. Ask volunteers to come to the SMART Board and show where the lines of symmetry are for each triangle, using the Lines tool. (They can rotate the triangles and the line.) Each time, encourage students to agree on whether or not the lines are correct, and ask them to suggest what type of triangle this is. Refer back to the names they agreed on earlier to check. Then use the Eraser from the Pen tray to erase the black marks to reveal the names of the triangles.

Independent Work

Give each student a copy of "Triangles" (p. 77). Divide the class into similar-ability groups. Ask less-confident learners to look for isosceles triangles and to find one line of symmetry in each. Confident learners can name and find lines of symmetry in all the triangles. Challenge more-confident learners to draw their own triangles with different numbers of lines of symmetry, using a mirror to check. They could also draw a triangle and ask another student to draw lines of symmetry.

Wrap-Up

Ask for a volunteer from each group to come up to the SMART Board and show where different types of triangles are on page 6 of the Notebook file, and to draw in the lines of symmetry. Refer back to the class definitions to agree with the groupings, and add the information about lines of symmetry for each type of triangle.

Nets

Getting Started

Give students these instructions:

Close your eyes. Imagine a square. "Draw" a diagonal line from one corner of the square to another. Visualize the triangles that are created by the diagonal line. Open your eyes. Draw the triangle on your individual whiteboard. In pairs, discuss what type of triangle you have drawn, and things you can say about it.

Take feedback from students, encouraging them to use the correct vocabulary. Make a note of key words on page 2 of the "Nets" Notebook file. Repeat the activity with a rectangle and discuss the differences.

Mini-Lesson

1. Explain to the class that they will be looking at how to make 3D shapes from 2D nets.

2. Display page 3 of the Notebook file. Ask: *What is a net?* (A flat pattern that can be cut and folded to create a 3-dimensional shape) Write correct definitions on the SMART Board. Explain to students that they will be designing their own net for a cube, and that this is the most common net they are likely to come across.

3. Use the squares on page 4 to create the standard cross design for a cube net. Discuss whether students have seen this net before—they may have used it to make dice, for example.

4. Break up the net and ask a volunteer to reconstruct it.

5. Demonstrate another possible net by moving one of the squares one place.

6. Display page 5 of the Notebook file, and ask if these nets would produce a cube. Tell students that there are over a dozen different nets for a cube using six squares.

7. Move one of the squares so that it would not be possible to make a cube from the net. Ask: *Why won't this net make a cube?*

Independent Work

Have students investigate drawing nets for a cube in order to identify as many variations as possible. They should work in pairs and put a question mark on any shapes that they think won't turn into nets. This is important for the Wrap-Up, as the shapes will be used, along with the correct nets, to identify common errors and strategies.

Wrap-Up

Invite students to recreate their nets on the SMART Board by moving the squares on page 6. Ask them to show a net that they think is correct and explain why it would work, and then another that they think is incorrect and to explain why. Try to fit both nets on one page. Draw conclusions about the right way to make a net. Formulate rules, such as: *The sides that are joined together should be the same size.* Print out the pages and model making up the nets if necessary.

Learning objectives

- Identify, visualize, and describe properties of rectangles, triangles, regular polygons, and 3D shapes.
- Use knowledge of properties to identify and draw nets of 3D shapes.

Resources

- "Nets" Notebook file
- individual whiteboards and pens

Whiteboard tools

- Pen tray
- Select tool

3D Shapes

Learning objective

- Make and draw shapes with increasing accuracy and apply knowledge of their properties.

Resources

- "3D Shapes" Notebook file
- models of 3D shapes (including a cube and rectangular prism)
- real-life examples of 3D shapes (such as cereal boxes, drinks cans, and balls)
- interlocking cubes

Whiteboard tools

- Pen tray
- Select tool
- Delete button
- Undo button

Getting Started

Start the lesson by asking students to complete the 3D shapes labeling activity on page 2 of the "3D Shapes" Notebook file, by dragging the names and dropping them under the appropriate shape. Distribute 3D examples of the shapes around the class. In groups, ask students whether these look different from the 3D images on the Notebook page. Ask questions such as: *How many faces does your 3D shape have? Can you tell this from the 2D drawing? How many vertices? What shape are the faces?*

Mini-Lesson

1. Show students the arrangement of cubes on page 3 of the Notebook file and explain that this shows two different views of the same object. Do students think it is difficult or easy to tell that they show the same object?

2. Give students, in groups, a set of interlocking cubes and ask them to make the shapes shown. Ask: *Can you see all of the cubes? How many cubes do you need to use?*

3. Ask students to hold up their shape when it is complete. Establish how many cubes were used to make the shape.

4. Go to page 4 and ask students to use their cubes to make the model shown on the Notebook page.

5. Ask students to draw a similar diagram of their model from a different viewpoint. Invite them to share their drawings.

Independent Work

Give students a choice of two different activities:

- Ask them to construct their own models using interlocking cubes, then to draw them on grid paper. Challenge more-confident learners to draw different views of the same model.

- Challenge students to investigate and draw all of the nets of a closed cube. Remind them of work they have done previously, involving nets of an open cube. Show them the examples on page 5 of the Notebook file to start them off. Provide less-confident learners with cardboard boxes to demonstrate nets.

Wrap-Up

Review all student work. If time is available, construct one or two of their examples on the SMART Board. Use page 6 to construct a 2D diagram of a model and page 7 to construct nets. (Press the Undo button to cancel the incorrect positioning of a square or cube. Use the Delete button to remove arrangements of shapes on page 6 and repeat the activity.) There is an infinite number of the shapes on these pages. Highlight any examples where it is not clear how many cubes were used to make a shape and ask: *Are there any cubes we cannot see?* Establish that there are 11 different nets of a closed cube. Invite volunteers to show their work before revealing the 11 different nets on page 8.

Finding Positions

Learning objective

- Describe and identify the position of a square on a grid of squares.

Resources

- "Finding Positions" Notebook file
- "Finding Coordinates" (p. 78)
- graph paper

Whiteboard tools

- Pen tray
- Lines tool
- Select tool

Getting Started

Display page 2 of the "Finding Positions" Notebook file. Discuss how positions where lines cross can be written as a coordinate, and the convention for doing this: (row, column). Use a phrase, such as: *Walk along the corridor and then go up or down the stairs*, to help students remember the order. Discuss and show students how to write the coordinate of the star.

Mark a chosen coordinate, such as (3, 2), with an X and ask: *What is the coordinate of this point?* Agree how this should be written. Invite a student to write the coordinate in the form (3, 2). Repeat for other coordinates.

Clear the page using the Eraser from the Pen tray (or press Edit and then Clear Page) and name a coordinate. Invite a student to mark with an X where it should be. Repeat for other coordinates.

Mini-Lesson

1. Display page 3 of the Notebook file, showing the map of an island. Invite students to describe what they can see on the map.

2. Ask for the coordinate of the treasure chest. Invite a student to write this next to the treasure chest icon beside the map.

3. Repeat for the other items on the map.

4. Now ask students to identify points where there is nothing on the map.

5. The icons on the map can be moved if you wish to check students' understanding of coordinates. For example, move the parrot to (5,1).

6. Return to page 2 of the Notebook file and delete the star. Mark an X at (5, 1) and explain that you want to draw a square, four squares high.

7. Ask: *What will the coordinate of the top of the line above (5, 1) be?* Mark the X and draw the line.

8. Repeat for the other two Xs and draw the lines.

9. Reset the page as before and repeat for drawing another shape.

Independent Work

Provide each student with a copy of "Finding Coordinates" (p. 78). Ask them to work individually to note the positions on the map.

Less-confident learners could use an 11" x 17" enlargement of the reproducible sheet and work together as a group. Encourage them to say the coordinates out loud, pointing to the row and column position each time.

Wrap-Up

Display page 4 of the Notebook file. Explain that you would like to draw a rectangle on the grid with sides that are three units in height and six units in length. Give a starting point of (1, 1) and ask students to suggest where the other Xs should go. Go to page 5, give a starting point of (1, 1), and this time draw a right triangle. The two sides containing the right angle should both be four units in length. Discuss how one side of the triangle is a diagonal line.

Coordinates

Learning objective

• Use all four quadrants to find coordinates of points determined by geometric information.

Resources

• "Coordinates" Notebook file
• "Plotting Coordinates" (p. 79)
• prepared "Plotting Coordinates" grid (p. 79) with questions covered

Whiteboard tools

• Pen tool
• Select tool
• Delete button

Getting Started

Go to page 2 of the "Coordinates" Notebook file. Encourage students to answer the questions: *What is a coordinate? What is a quadrant?* Write their responses on the Notebook page. Use the *Coordinates Interactive Teaching Program* to demonstrate coordinates to students. Click on the icon with the crosshair to make it appear on the grid along with its coordinates. Move the crosshair around the grid and tell students to pay attention to how the coordinate changes.

Mini-Lesson

1. Using the diagram on page 3 of the Notebook file, discuss the four quadrants. Think of a way for students to remember how to use the *x*-axis before the *y*-axis (for example, *along the corridor and up or down the stairs*).

2. Work through pages 3 to 10 of the Notebook file, encouraging students to place the items on the correct coordinates.

3. Prompt them with suitable probing questions. For example: *In which quadrant is the comet?* or *How would the coordinate change if we moved the object two places down?*

4. Consider what would happen if you read the coordinates the wrong way round. Demonstrate this, using one of these pages.

Independent Work

Give each student a copy of "Plotting Coordinates" (p. 79) and ask students to follow the instructions on the sheet. Provide support for less-confident learners.

After working through the questions, give each student a blank grid (photocopy the worksheet with the questions covered). Arrange for students to work in pairs. Challenge them to plot six stars on their grid without their partner seeing. Have them take turns guessing their partner's coordinates. As an extra challenge, invite some students to present their coordinates to the whole class using the blank grid on page 11 of the Notebook file.

Wrap-Up

Go to page 12 of the Notebook file and invite students to answer the questions that were posed at the beginning of the session: *What is a coordinate? Which coordinate comes first in the sequence?* Discuss any misconceptions during this section and work out any difficult areas on the board.

Pictograms

Learning objectives
- Answer a question by identifying what data to collect.
- Organize, present, analyze, and interpret the data in tally charts and pictograms.

Resources
- "Pictogram" Notebook file

Whiteboard tools
- Pen tray
- Select tool
- Lines tool
- On-screen Keyboard
- Capture tool

Getting Started
Display page 2 of the "Pictogram" Notebook file. Write in a survey question, such as: *What pets do you have?* Agree how to collect the data: for example, by recording the number of students who have dogs, cats, or rabbits. Draw a simple data-collection chart and enter the information using tallies. (Use the Lines tool to draw charts and a Pen from the Pen tray to enter the tally.)

Go to page 3 of the Notebook file and repeat for another question, such as: *What is your favorite type of day out?* Record the number of students who like museums, theme parks, water parks, and so on.

Mini-Lesson
1. Put students into mixed-ability groups of about four. Tell them that they are going to gather data from other students. (The quantity of data needs to be large, so agree with other teachers that students can come to their classes in small groups to ask their questions.)

2. Display page 4 of the Notebook file. Encourage each group to think of a survey question (for example, month of birth or number of brothers or sisters). Write notes and suggestions on the Notebook file if required.

3. Discuss and agree how students should collect their data. They should make a tally chart and agree on the fields (or headings) before they begin.

Independent Work
Students should collect their data and total it for each field. Encourage more-confident learners to provide support for those who are less confident, if necessary.

Wrap-Up
Pick one of the groups to share their data. Go to page 5 of the Notebook file. Press the button to open the pictogram. Discuss what the headings for each row should be and type these in. (Use the On-screen Keyboard to add headings to the empty pictogram.) Discuss how many items one symbol should stand for. Explain that you cannot use a symbol to represent every single item. For example, in many pictograms a symbol represents 10 or even 20 items. Ask students to calculate how many symbols are needed for each heading and input these. Discuss how to complete the row where the items do not divide exactly by the number of units chosen for each symbol. Fill in the key box. Use the Capture tool to insert a screenshot of the finished pictogram on a new Notebook page.

Ask questions about the data, such as: *How many more ___ are there than ___? Which is the most/least popular? How can you tell that?* Encourage students to speculate about their data. Ask: *How accurate do you think is this data? Why do you think that? How could we improve on our data collection?* Use the data collected by other groups in subsequent lessons.

Bar Charts

Learning objectives
- Suggest a line of inquiry and the strategy needed to follow it.
- Collect, organize, and interpret selected information to find answers.

Resources
- "Bar Charts" Notebook file
- small safety mirrors
- large sheets of construction paper

Whiteboard tools
- Pen tray
- Highlighter pen
- Select tool
- Undo button
- On-screen Keyboard

Getting Started
Open page 2 of the "Bar Charts" Notebook file and prompt students with questions to analyze the bar chart and the data that it represents. (Use a Highlighter pen to draw attention to data in the bar charts.) *What is the title of this bar chart? What do you think it will tell us? What is the scale? How many students went to ___ for vacation? Which was the most/least popular destination? How many fewer/more students went to ___ than ___? If everybody went on vacation, how many students are in the school?*

Mini-Lesson
1. Discuss the survey question on page 3 of the Notebook file.
2. Give each student a small safety mirror. Ask them to count their own teeth and make a note of the result.
3. Discuss how to gather the data. Students could put their hands up if they have 20 teeth, 21 teeth, and so on.
4. When the data has been gathered, reveal the blank bar chart on page 4. Ask students to suggest the title and axis headings. Use the On-screen Keyboard to type in the suggested headings.
5. Discuss what scale should be used, and why. (This is likely to be in twos or fives, but will depend upon the data gathered.) Use the Select tool to alter the height of the bars in the bar chart. Discuss any data that needs a fraction of a bar and how this can be represented.
6. Discuss the data and highlight comparisons. Ask questions, such as: *How many students have ___ teeth? Are there more/fewer students with ___ teeth than ___?*

Independent Work
Ask students to work in mixed-ability groups of four or five. Each group will collect data about the color of the family car from a different class in the school. (You will need to discuss this with the relevant teachers beforehand.) Students should agree how to collect the data and what the headings on their tally chart should be. Once they have collected the data, they should use it to make a bar chart on large sheets of construction paper. They should agree on the scale, the title, and the axis headings. Allow one group to use the bar chart file on page 4 of the Notebook file. Encourage more-confident learners to support those who are less confident.

Wrap-Up
Invite each group, in turn, to show their data. Use the Undo button to reset the bar chart on page 4 of the Notebook file to compile a collective bar chart, using all of the data that students have collected. Invite students to suggest axis headings, scale, and title. Ask questions about the data, such as: *How many more red than blue cars are there? Which is the most popular color? How would the chart look if we changed the scale to ___? Would this be helpful? Why/Why not? Is the data from each class the same? Why not?* Make a note of students' observations on page 5 of the Notebook file.

Analyzing Data

Getting Started

Display page 2 of the "Analyzing Data" Notebook file. Ask students to state division facts derived from the number sentence shown. Record these facts and prompt the use of patterns to extend the range of facts. Go to page 3 and repeat the activity, this time stating multiplication facts.

Mini-Lesson

1. Explain to students that they will be looking at the average monthly temperatures during the year for New York. From this data they are going to find:
   - the *mean* (the average number when all the data is added together then divided by the total number of entries)
   - the *range* (the difference between the lowest and highest numbers)
   - the *mode* (the number that appears most often)
   - the *median* (the central number when all the data has been put into order from smallest to largest)

2. Review these meanings on page 4 of the Notebook file. Then display page 5, which shows the average monthly temperature for one year in New York.

3. Using the four definitions, the class should begin to organize the temperatures from coldest to warmest in order to find the range, then the mode, mean, and median temperatures.

4. Identify the range by finding the difference between the coldest and warmest temperatures. Ask: *How would you calculate this if the coldest temperature was –6°F?*

5. Next, identify the mode. Explain that if two sets of numbers appear equally then they are both the mode numbers.

6. Identify the mean number by adding all 12 entries and dividing by 12.

7. Identify the median number. When there is an odd set of figures (seven, for example), then the middle number is the median number. In this case there are two median numbers; to find the absolute median, the two numbers need to be added together and divided by 2.

Independent Work

Explain that students are going to be presented with a range of temperatures taken from other countries (using Notebook page 6). Their task is to find the mean, mode, median, and range of each city and to present this as a table in their notebooks.

Wrap-Up

Discuss the strategies used and identify the most efficient ways of finding the four results. Remind students that it is very important to organize the list of numbers before starting the activity, as this will help with finding the median, range, and mode. If time permits, use page 7 of the Notebook file to compare the data from the Independent Work (on London) with the data from the Mini-Lesson work (on New York). Review students' work, making notes on page 8 of the Notebook file if necessary.

Learning objective
- Describe and interpret results and solutions to problems using the mode, range, median, and mean.

Resources
- "Analyzing Data" Notebook file
- writing materials
- individual whiteboards and pens

Whiteboard tools
- Pen tray
- Highlighter pen
- Select tool

Name _____ Date _____

A Place for Each Digit

Work with a partner. You will need a set of 0 to 9 number cards.

- Take turns choosing four cards.
- Each of you makes a four-digit integer with the cards.
  (Try to make your integers different!)
- Record your integer and each digit's place value in the grid below.
- Do this nine more times.

Integer	Thousands	Hundreds	Tens	Ones

Now write your integers again, this time using words.

1. _____
2. _____
3. _____
4. _____
5. _____
6. _____
7. _____
8. _____
9. _____
10. _____

Math Lessons for the SMART Board: Grades 4–6 © 2011, Scholastic